2

Minding my Peas AND Cucumbers

Quirky Tales of ALLOTMENT LIFE

Minding my Peas AND Cucumbers

Quirky Tales OF ALLOTMENT LIFE

Kay Sexton

summersdale

MINDING MY PEAS AND CUCUMBERS

Summersdale Publishers Ltd
46 West Street
Chichester
West Sussex
PO19 1RP
UK

www.summersdale.com

Printed and bound in Great Britain

ISBN: 978-1-84953-135-1

Contents

Note from the Author

When I was two I started digging up my parents' back garden with a soup spoon. A year later, when we moved, you could have created a fair-sized swimming pool in the hole I'd manufactured. It was my first, but by no means last, digging marathon.

In my teens and twenties I travelled round the world, working in a variety of jobs: all glamorous, many fascinating, but none of them stable enough to allow me to put down roots. I watched my parents create garden after garden, and planned to do the same myself, but somehow I was always on the move again after a year or so. My Other Half had always 'grown his own', so when we married and he joined my vagabond lifestyle he managed to find room for a couple of tomato plants or some herbs, wherever we lived. Or house plants... we had a lot of house plants.

We eventually settled back in the UK and I stopped doing glamorous jobs and took up saving the world as a career. It meant working even longer hours and travelling to conferences where earnest people talked about the imminent collapse of just about everything, from the water table to the upper atmosphere. I attended conferences and symposia across the UK, arguing for whichever bit of the planet I was currently responsible for trying to save, and stared out of train windows at other people's allotments on my journeys home. Whenever I could, I volunteered myself as an allotment helper, all the time longing for one of my own.

By the time I was thirty I had a small child in tow and a settled job, administering a think-tank researching global problems. We moved to a suburban house with a garden which I planted with the pent-up passion of three decades of horticultural deprivation. OH, already green-fingered, developed his skills as a garden constructor and together we created a green space that rivalled the gardens that were open to the public for charity – in fact, by the end of the decade I was running a tree planting charity and even opened my garden one day a year to raise funds – but there was something missing...

Gardening had become a competitive activity and an expensive one too, costing us both money and what little time we had free from commuting or family time. The fun had gone; our green space became another room that required constant cleaning and housekeeping, upkeep and maintenance. There were still a few herbs tucked into corners, but they were mainly the decorative kind. I couldn't bear to sacrifice more than a few inches of soil to the humdrum needs of vegetables. I certainly didn't have the time or enthusiasm to be working on other people's allotments any more.

At forty I had a new career as a stay-at-home writer and my teenage son no longer required much adult supervision. A client asked me to write an article about allotments and for the first time in years I went to an allotment site... and it was as if I'd been given back my soup spoon!

It took years to get a plot of our own. Sometimes we wondered if it would ever happen, but getting to know the people on our local allotment sites and being invited to work with them on their plots made the wait not just bearable but utterly enjoyable. This book is for them and about them, although names and places have been changed to protect those who shared their crops and their stories so freely. It's also for OH, who quietly puts up with all my horticultural passions and helps bring my greenest ambitions to life, and for my parents, who gave me the soup spoon...

Learning My Plot
and My Place

For many people, living on a nudist holiday complex in the South of France would be a dream come true, but all the time I lived there, my dreams were about allotments. It was the sunflowers and lavender fields that did it: those sun-following golden sentinels, alternating with vast expanses of fragrant purple billows like a sea of scent made tangible. I was living in a white-painted concrete box, piled up in a jumble of other concrete boxes overlooking an ocean that was so dazzlingly bright on a sunny morning it could sear your eyeballs. Each morning I drove inland to teach yoga to Parisian women who were renting summer villas near Perpignan, and with every mile that I moved from tourist haven to rural isolation, I became more enchanted with the idea of growing my own fruit and vegetables.

The French gardens, filled with gleaming produce, sleepy cats and sun-bleached hammocks, looked like small squares of heaven. The French gardeners, arms full of courgettes or fennel or sipping *pastis* as the sun set over their productive land, looked as if they had found answers to questions – both horticultural and philosophical – that I hadn't even learned to formulate. My concrete box neighbour had an elderly mother who visited him (the only fully clothed inhabitant of our naked village) and cooked *soupe au pistou*, rich with basil and summer vegetables. She passed bowls over the concrete wall and OH and I agreed that her cooking tasted even better than the *haute cuisine* we ate with gastronomic French friends. The sunflowers and lavender sealed a desire that had burgeoned as the vines filled and the pumpkins swelled and when I returned to the UK I got onto the waiting list for an allotment. And waited. And waited…

After a few years, we moved. And joined another waiting list. And waited. And waited…

On my daily commute across London, or from Sussex to London, I saw allotments: lovely ones with brick paths, full of shining fruit; neglected ones, chin-deep in nettles and brambles, with wistful sheds; utilitarian ones with concrete paths and bunker-like compost bins and serried ranks of regimented vegetables. I yearned. I whined. And finally I got off my backside and did something about it. I became a co-worker. It allowed me to pretend I was an allotment-holder. And after a couple of years, I got an allotment – sort of…

About eight months later, on a particularly torrid August evening, the plants were drought-stricken and drooping. The problem was at least half mine. I'd planted an immense number of things I would never get around to eating because I hadn't expected all of them to come up. OH reckoned that when he was a boy, half the seeds he'd planted had failed to come up and half the ones that came up had been eaten by slugs, so we'd sown our crops on that basis. Everything, but everything, had come up: I'd been giving away cucumbers for three weeks, and neighbours were starting to pretend they weren't home when I knocked on their doors. I was sometimes tempted to post cucumbers through letterboxes, but so far I'd restrained myself.

It was just too awful to think about throwing away perfectly good fresh vegetables, although I had almost begun to cry when I'd opened the fridge and found that the six lettuces I was holding wouldn't fit inside because there were eight lettuces there already. And nobody in my house even likes lettuce very much.

So I'd already learned a harsh lesson about gluts and my inability to be ruthless with green stuff, and I was about to learn a harsher one about my place in the allotment pecking order...

I was waiting to use the tap attached to the water tank, from which hosepipes could be run. Although the water butt on the plot had been empty for nearly a week, it gave off a rank, rotting smell out of all proportion to the tiny amount of weed and algae that it contained. I'd found it was better to stay away from that corner of the plot as the odour could make your eyes swim. On this site, with more than 300 allotments and many time-poor allotment-holders trying to use the water tanks at the same time, water butts were not so much a valuable item as an absolute necessity, and water butts – or the lack of – were going to continue to play a big role in my life for the next few years. For now though, as a relatively new plot-manager, on a clay soil over chalk subsoil allotment, all I knew about water was that if the allotment didn't get it, the plants died and if the allotment got too much, it flooded. The only other thing I knew was that the allotment committee, who'd given me this plot to manage, would be expecting me to keep those plants alive, and I couldn't afford to fail. I'd read the allotment regulations and I knew I had a lot of rules to keep. Not least the rule about dogs being under control, which meant I'd left Rebus, the allotment terrier, at home because it he thought that hosepipes were a form of amusement for hot dogs and I didn't think his hysterical barking as he tried to bite the jet of water would be considered a valuable addition to allotment life.

An allotment-holder from about four or five plots away was using the tap for his hose, but he'd been connected for an hour already, so I didn't think I'd have to wait too much longer. I'd said hello as I passed and asked how his sweet peas were doing, before commenting that my lettuces were prostrate with heat exhaustion and looking forward to a cool drink. He wasn't exactly chatty, but that was fairly standard for the older male allotment-holder, many of whom viewed newcomers with an ironic disdain that said they'd seen newbies come and go, while they trudged on. Trudging was part of the old-guard style, as was wearing a tank-top girded over an old shirt with a leather belt. The old-guard chaps accessorised their look with a roll-up stuck to their bottom lip, and ensured everything they owned was stained the same dull brown by the Sussex clay which could glue you to the ground on a wet day. They were quietly amused by the silly ideas of the 'weekend growers' who took on an allotment in summer and lost interest by winter. I was determined to prove this member of the fraternity wrong. I might be new to this site, but I wasn't a total newbie, oh no! I knew my way around an allotment and I would win his respect or die trying.

An hour later I was still waiting to use the tap and I didn't have a clue what I should do about it.

The tanks were meant for communal use, so I knew I had every right to go and ask him to disconnect his hose so I could use mine – but I didn't have the nerve. I'd tried dropping another hint, by walking the hundred yards from my plot to the tank with two watering cans, filling the cans by plunging them in the tank, walking back to my plot and emptying them around the wilting courgettes, but he appeared immune to the idea that my curious behaviour might have anything to do with him. Perhaps, I thought, he believed I was choosing to act like sweated labour – it was possible that, to a man in his seventies, my trudging to and fro with two green plastic cans looked like the latest form of aerobics. I'd seen people do stupider-looking things with balls and hoops and bands in the gym. So I stopped. Instead I went and pinched out the tops of my runner bean plants, which were trying to anchor themselves to nothing but the deep blue sky of a summer's evening. It was fiddly work, but it at least stopped the growth of the plant, encouraging it instead to produce more beans. When I'd finished, watering man was still watering.

I took my hosepipe up to the tank and left it there. He couldn't ignore that.

He did.

I spent another twenty minutes weeding – pulling out the endless streamers of bindweed that I knew were going to bedevil me for at least another five years – and then wandered up to the tank, toying casually with my hose connector and rehearsing a chummy comment about wanting to use the standpipe. He was standing with his back to me, soaking the red-veined leaves of four rows of beetroot. What a bloody waste of water, I thought. Doesn't he know that he needs to water the soil, not the leaves? I coughed. He put his thumb over the end of the hose and squirted the resulting spray around the base of his apple tree. It looked obscenely like the *Manneken Pis* but without the charm of the little statue in Brussels.

Losing my nerve I retreated to my plot and filled in some time hunting down the manky strawberries I'd failed to harvest when they were just ripe and which now threatened to spread grey rot to their neighbours.

Three hours after I first wanted to use the tank, my neighbour coiled up his hose and retreated to his greenhouse. I ran over and shoved my connector onto the tap, to ensure I was the next user – a bit like the apocryphal German and the sun-lounger towel – then I rolled out my hose before turning on the water. You learn that lesson very quickly: a full hosepipe is heavy, so if you turn the water on and then trundle the hose back to your plot, you are at least trebling the effort. And if you leave your hose snaking out, empty, from the tank to your plot, people drive over it and damage it, and other people come along and yell at you for causing a hazard and tripping them up as they stroll home with a trug full of peas or currants.

I had water! And as I trotted back to my plot, my neighbour passed me, whistling tunelessly. He walked as if he didn't see me, as if I didn't exist. It was now almost dark, and as I squinted to see the plants against the twilight, I wondered what I should have done. If I'd had any guts at all, then I would have simply gone up to the hosepipe hog and asked how much longer he expected to be, because other people were waiting. But I knew that if I'd done that, it would have been a declaration of a war that I could never win. He was one of the 'real' allotment-holders who'd been on the site since the 1960s, and I was a mimsy newcomer: the kind of 'Sunday gardener' that the real allotment people loathed and laughed at. I knew enough to know not to cross the old guard, even if I didn't know how to handle disputes with them.

Long before being granted a plot to manage, I'd been co-opted as Allotment Society secretary which gave me an inside view of allotment life and allowed me to observe the old-time committee members laying bets on how long some novice would last – they were never out by more than a month. I wasn't sure how much of their ability to predict the departure of a new allotment-holder was prescience and how much was their tendency to twist situations to drive novices away. When newbies came into our allotment shop to buy barrowloads of manure, or seeds, or just to seek advice, the old guard would look them over like gamblers betting on a horse race. For the newcomer it must have been like the first day at school, having to learn the rules, jargon and arcane behaviours required to fit in as an outsider. It was something I hadn't been much good at when I first started my allotment quest, nearly a decade earlier, but I was determined to manage it this time.

The immediate solution was obvious. I stood in the dark, two hours late for dinner, listening to my mobile phone warbling away in the shed as my family rang to find out if I'd emigrated or suffered some appalling allotment-based accident, and filled the stinking butt with water from the tank. If I had to spend another night irrigating my plot with watering cans, I would at least do it from my own water supply. And I was determined not to let that miserable man defeat me – not a single lettuce would be lost, nor a bean blighted, through his behaviour!

I got home after ten to a dark house and a snippy note on the kitchen counter pointing out that an allotment was supposed to improve the quality of life, not take over every waking hour. 'You spend more time up there than you did with your son when he was a baby,' was OH's parting shot. It was probably true, but nobody had tried to prevent my access to the baby, and there had been no suggestion that I could lose my infant if he wasn't in perfect condition whenever some crusty old cultivator came to look at him. As a new mum I'd been confident – as a new allotment-holder I was not. Confidence came over the next few years and, like any mum, I got through the teething problems somehow. One day I looked around and realised that not only did I know what I was doing, I was really enjoying doing it. I didn't have a tank-top, or a roll-up glued to my lip, but I was considered to be one of the 'old guard', and I did, finally, know a lot of the answers. I had found my place on the plot.

There's Never a Good Day to Get an Allotment

By which I mean that whatever the time of year you are offered a plot will turn out to be a bad time. If you take on your plot in spring, the weeds get away from you faster than you can get to them, and each time you visit less of your plot is visible under the mounds of bindweed, carpets of couch grass and thickets of bramble. Your neighbours will have neat rows of early potatoes, peas like filigree and broad beans as sturdy and neat as Montessori children. They will also have pitying expressions that become more judgemental each time you try, and fail, to get to grips with your perennial weed problem.

In autumn, on the other hand, you'll find that every visit reveals a new grim truth that the growth of summer had hidden. The cute brick path turns out to be a slippery, uneven death trap when it rains. The shed roof leaks, and a small stream appears to meander underneath it, meaning that the upward rising and downward falling damp patches meet just at the point where the lock is, so that the permanently warped door refuses to open when you arrive or close when you leave.

Get your plot in summer and it will lull you into a false sense of security, so that instead of tearing almost everything out or down, as you'd intended, you lounge around, harvesting perennial fruits planted by a previous incumbent and feeling at peace with the world, and then autumn happens and an allotment officer pitches up to point out, severely, that your plot is not adequately cultivated and you have a month to do all the things you should have spent the past three months doing. Of course, on some sites there isn't an allotment officer and you can just let your plot lie fallow while you enjoy the sunshine, but increasingly allotments are being patrolled by zealous officers and covetous wannabe allotment-holders who get on the case of anybody who seems to be failing to meet high horticultural standards.

And in winter... well, taking on an allotment in the dead months is a bit like being in a zombie movie – the whole place is dead, there seems to nobody around to advise you, and there are a few suspicious-looking twigs on an otherwise bare plot that could be plants, or weeds, or the gnarled fingers of a spectacularly gothic but poorly buried corpse. These skeletal fingers will probably turn out to be rhubarb, and in this case you will be digging up rhubarb plantlets for the next five years, and wishing they had in fact been a corpse because at least that way the forensic team would have done the digging for you.

At this low point in your allotment initiation, the zombies do arrive, silent and shambling, trundling past you in a slow wave of green-wellied stoicism, and you start to wonder if you've strayed into a horror story. The reality is that all the allotment-holders who have free travel passes tend to arrive on the same bus, particularly on Sundays: it's the over-sixties contingent arriving en masse. Nobody seems to tell newcomers any of this. Books and TV programmes never mention the deep gloom that will overcome you from time to time when you contemplate the weeds, pests and crop failures associated with your allotment, or the daydreams you will have about giving it up and spending the weekend on the sofa with a box set of DVDs and no reason to go out and dig or weed in the rain.

Nowhere does it say that a relationship with fruit and veg is as difficult as a marriage, and as prone to patches of despair, even if it does generally turn out to be rewarding in the end. And it's never the struggling allotment-holders who get to raise their voices on *Gardeners' Question Time*, so you can easily feel you're the only one who's failing.

This is when a lot of people give up, which is a shame, because the rewards are just around the corner: the first crops appear and are delicious; the surly characters who used to ignore you now exchange cheery greetings; a fellow allotment-holder pays you a compliment on your work – suddenly you feel that you fit in and you're doing a good job. Getting through 'getting started' can take a while, but it's great when you finally feel at home on your plot.

'Getting started' involves two things that need to happen simultaneously: showing you're bringing the plot into proper cultivation is one, and spending time looking at it and learning about it so you can make good decisions in the future is the other. The former, in your first year, is probably best thought of as a 'fake it until you make it' approach to growing, while the latter involves poking around in the corners of your plot and trying to work out what the last plot-holder actually intended to do with the bidet they plonked near the shed, or whether the raspberry canes can be pruned back to productivity before you bleed to death by a thousand prickles.

Faking can be the quickest way to get into productivity, especially on a neglected plot. Be warned, however. You can strim and rotovate and make it look as if you've got a perfect growing base, but the soil will still be suffering from whatever lacks and losses it has experienced during its non-productive period. This means that the crops you plant with such high hopes are likely to be spindly/blighted/eaten by pests/swamped by weeds and you will become discouraged and mope around like Ophelia in rubber boots or like Hamlet with a hoe.

When I began work on my first allotment it had been strimmed and rotovated. The soil looked like the plastic furrows that had been part of the toy farm I'd loved when I was four years old: each tiny plastic furrow had contained a row of holes into which I could insert plastic cabbages, carrots, or some round and vaguely vegetable-shaped things that were possibly meant to be miniature marrows, or maybe giant gooseberries. In my optimism I had a similar approach to the allotment: dib a hole, drop in a seed, and hey presto! I would be rewarded with perfectly shaped, beautifully regular, shiny cabbages, carrots and mutant globular things like those in my toy farm set. Unconsciously, I think I also believed that getting an allotment was a sign of maturity, and that once my mutant harvest was brought home, I would be granted understanding of its nature and of how to cook it, as if a good fairy had just waved the wand of culinary adulthood over me.

What I actually got was five summer cabbages, two of which were so hollowed out by caterpillars that only the ribs remained, zero carrots and one hideously shaped marrow which had rotted at the blossom end before it filled out properly – it could easily be described as mutant, but not in the way I'd been hoping for.

In year two I faked it. By which I mean my long-suffering Other Half made me some raised beds, which were just lengths of scavenged decking sunk into the ground so that the wood was around fifteen centimetres proud of the soil. I weeded these wooden boxes and filled them with a mixture of compost/manure/top soil into which I planted carrots and a squash plant. Apart from being geographically 'on' the allotment, there was no real relationship between most of the plants I grew and the plot I was supposedly growing them on. I also grew cabbages in the ground, but under fleece. This time I got loads of squashes, and all my cabbages, and zero carrots.

In year three I put a six-inch fleece 'fence' around the top of a raised bed to stop carrot fly, and harvested more carrots than we could eat even with me serving carrot cake twice a day, plus a glut of squashes… and only half the cabbages I'd planted, because the slugs had worked out how to get under the fleece.

In year four I realised all the raised beds were in the wrong place. They were also too close together and needed to be a different size and shape.

The raised beds were an answer, but not the best one. What I should really have used in those first years were some containers: old buckets, battered planters, maybe a trough or two… things I could have dragged around to relocate my plants as the patterns of sun and shade, wind and rain became evident over the seasons. Containers would have given me portability along with productivity – I would have been growing my own, without committing myself or my plants to putting down permanent roots.

 ## Container Planting

So, if fast and argument-free crops are a priority for you, begging, borrowing or bodging together a bunch of containers can be the easiest answer. They allow you to get fruit and vegetable harvests within six months of taking over your plot, without having to work the soil until your back and bank balance break.

You can be resourceful about the containers you use: I know one allotment-holder who grows his garlic in an old car roof box, opened flat and with drainage holes drilled in the base! I grow watercress in a cracked porcelain shower base that a local DIY store let me buy for a pound. Don't forget to check the rules for your allotment site though – some are pickier than others about what you can bring onto your plot. For example, nearly all sites now ban car tyres because they are toxic and non-biodegradable.

What you can grow depends on the depth of your container – make sure you leave a couple of inches at the top to allow for watering and the fact that root crops in particular will 'heave' and displace the soil around their crowns, so that they risk standing proud of the earth. It's better to leave room in case you need to top them up with some more compost or soil to cover their shoulders.

- In ten centimetres of soil you can grow lettuce, pak choi, radishes, chives, Welsh onions, basil, coriander, marjoram.

- In fifteen centimetres of soil you can plant dwarf beans, garlic, kohlrabi, smaller onions and shallots, dwarf peas, mint (best to give this a permanent container of its own because it's invasive), summer savoury, thyme and nasturtiums.

- With thirty centimetres of soil you can really go to town: aubergines, beetroot, runner beans and cabbage, carrots, chard, chillies, courgettes, cucumber (better under cover if possible), chicory, fennel, leeks, peppers, spinach, dwarf sweetcorn, tomatoes and turnips will all grow for you.

- You can even put some perennial fruit in containers of this depth, so choose from melons (but they do need specialist conditions), black, red and white currants, gooseberries, raspberries (they'll need supports), rhubarb, blueberries (they may not like you as much as you like them: they can be fussy about climate) and strawberries.

- The more complex herbs can be planted to this depth too, so you can have containers full of bay, borage, dill, fennel, lemon balm, lovage, parsley (I have no idea why parsley requires such a deep planter, but it won't thrive in a shallower one), rosemary, sage and tarragon.

🦋 Crops that you just can't grow in a container, unless you are superlatively green-fingered, are asparagus, broad beans, celery/celeriac, parsnips, potatoes (it's easy to grow spuds in specialist containers, but not necessarily in tubs or buckets), fruit trees and grapevines, blackberries, loganberries and tayberries.

Container growing is cheating, no doubt about it, because it doesn't teach you anything about the ground you've been given to work with. But it gives you time to learn and think and plan, and if you're committing to a long-term relationship with your plot, it's better to learn, think and plan before you do anything it could be costly and difficult to undo later.

The other great advantage of container-grown crops, in your first year, is that you can control more of the conditions. It's true you may have to water more, but your soil fertility should be guaranteed and while you may have to wrestle with slugs, snails, aphids and butterflies, you are at least spared the vicious sneak attacks of soil-borne nasties like eelworms, vine weevils and the depredations of keel slugs which go through a root crop like Attila the Hun through a sleeping village.

I remember the day we ate our first allotment-grown crops. The owner of the Koh-i-noor diamond, presenting it to his beloved as a token of his esteem, could not have been prouder than me as I handed OH a washed bunch of radishes.

He looked at them with extreme distaste. 'What's this?'

'Radishes.' My tone probably lacked a certain brightness, given his negative response to the evidence of our labours.

'Radishes are red. Round and red.' He tried to give me back the handful of pendant white roots, and we were launched on one of our periodic rows about what is, and isn't, a crop. OH is usually relaxed about food, and can be positively evangelical. It was his idea to grow asparagus peas, for example, and his insistence that there must be some good way to cook the pretty but tough-textured crop led to seven separate attempts to make them edible before we gave up. On the other hand, he has a bit of a blind spot when it comes to traditional foods. In OH's world, carrots are orange, radishes are red, cabbages are round and apples grow on trees above your head not on step-overs the height of his knee. Crops he remembers from his childhood have to look the way they did when his father brought them in from the garden or his sense of fittingness is somehow violated and he feels uncomfortable.

I've learned, over the years, to cook new versions of traditional vegetables before he ever gets to see them as a raw ingredient. In this way he's become familiar with chocolate-brown peppers, yellow tomatoes, round carrots and sausage-shaped pumpkins.

The radishes – which were Snow Belle: a porcelain white and perfectly globular variety that's particularly good for salads – languished in the fridge for a day or two before I worked out how to sneak them under his food radar and make him eat them, and enjoy them, without realising it. The answer was Pizzicato.

Pizzicato means that a note on a stringed instrument is played with the finger rather than the bow to produce a different sound: short and rapid rather than sustained. The radish is a pizzicato crop in both growth and flavour.

Summer radishes can be ready in five weeks from sowing. This means that if you are given a plot around four weeks before 21 June, you can be eating your first crop in just over a month.

After 21 June, as the day length shortens, you are likely to get an odd-tasting harvest: radishes become extremely hot, very pungent or woody either because you leave them too long before harvesting, or because they have poor soil or not enough water, but also because sowing them after the longest day means they don't get enough daylight to allow them to develop properly. If you grow them in containers before 21 June, your radishes should always be moist, peppery and delicious.

The winter radish is an entirely different animal, a slow-growth crop that's becoming increasingly popular in the UK. It is planted almost as soon as you have to stop planting the summer variety and has longer, deeper roots, like a carrot, that may be white, red or black depending on variety. It tastes like an assertive turnip when boiled – a bit peppery, a bit crunchy, not at all inclined to shrink into the background of a dish – or it can be pickled in vinegar to produce a delicacy, much prized in Japan, called takuan.

RADISH PIZZICATO

INGREDIENTS

- 12 or so thumb-sized summer radishes

- 2 cloves garlic

- 200 grams soft spreadable cheese

- Seasoning

- A good-sized bunch of fresh herbs (enough to sit on the palm of your hand): parsley, marjoram, thyme, dill, chives, tarragon – more or less whatever you have to hand, but stay away from basil and mint, both of which overpower the peppery and bright taste of the radish

METHOD

Whiz the first four ingredients together in a food processor, or finely chop by hand, then hand-chop the herbs to remove any woody stalks and blend them into the mixture with your fingers.

Put in a dish and refrigerate for at least two hours. Serve with hot cheese scones, wholemeal bread or melba toast.

The Natural History of Allotment-Holders

Allotments are fascinating and deserve their own documentary series. The sites alone are complex sociological melting pots and the habits and beliefs of allotment-holders are a peculiar blend of mythology, thoroughly tested local tips and profoundly developed obsessions. Add in the history and archaeology, flora and fauna, feuds, competitions and culinary expertise and there's enough material to keep a researcher busy for decades – or until they get an allotment of their own and lose all interest in outside matters. Each site is peculiar (in every sense of the word) and particular, with conditions, rules, traditions and crops specifically designed for that ground.

Village allotments, for example, tend to be like libraries: anybody can get in, but usually only the old, the lonely and self-improvers actually do. In library terms, these are the people who do the *Times* crossword to exercise their brains – in allotment terms they are self-sufficiency enthusiasts. City allotments are much more like theme parks: the queues to get in are long, the cost is high and people are grimly determined to have fun.

People who obtain a city allotment, if allowed enough time, will usually sort themselves out. They arrive as loud and demanding family groups and shake down to a single individual, almost never the actual plot tenant, who will quietly, slowly, often painfully, become a dedicated grower. The beefy young dad with his ear-splitting rotovator will appear three weekends in a row with his barbecue, lager and cronies, and from then on, his wife, pushing the baby in a buggy, cajoling the toddler along, and with her hand tools in amongst the nappies and juice bottles, will be the only person who visits the plot, spending hours multi-tasking her crops and her kids.

Every year there's a bossy woman in paisley wellingtons, who turns up with a car full of cuttings, monogrammed pruning implements and adult children with aspirational names: 'Iolanthe, could you please put down your phone and lay the pot-herbs out in a pleasing design. Jasper, stop sulking and help your father with the hazel hurdles.' After a few weeks, she will vanish. In her place a silent son- or daughter-in-law, Tim or Sarah or Peter or Becky, will almost invisibly develop the plot, and their own self-confidence, until one day they are the whole site's 'go to' person for brassica hints or grafting fruit trees and their plot causes newcomers to stand and gaze, saying 'That's what I want. How long does it take to get your plot looking so good?' And Tim or Sarah or Peter or Becky will try, very gently, to explain that looks are a by-product of good growing conditions and experience, but the new arrival won't listen, and drags his or her sulking, quarrelling, resentful family off to their own plot to start slash and burn agriculture. As they bicker and yell, it seems wholly impossible that anybody in that already bitter and disgruntled group could become a dedicated allotment-holder, but – given time – somebody often will.

Except nobody is given time these days; thirty, sixty or ninety days and you're out if you haven't cultivated enough of your plot, cleared all the rubbish, put up your plot number, strimmed the perennially seeding weeds, or whatever else the council and/ or allotment committee considers to be key criteria for 'good' allotment-holders. And while there are many wonderful books about allotments, most don't seem to deal with the problems I, and many other new allotment-holders, faced, which is why I wanted to write a book that dealt with the questions that had troubled me when I first got involved in allotments.

When I started managing my first plot for an absentee tenant (with a second home in Provence, a daughter in Maine, a sister in New Zealand and frequent flier miles up to her oxters – not that I was at all envious!) I was given, or I begged, borrowed or bought, a shelf of books on growing fruit and vegetables which caused more fury than enlightenment in my heart because they seemed to be written by full-time growers for people who had perfect soil, unlimited time and substantial disposable income.

I, on the other hand (calloused from wielding mattock and hoe), had weedy, neglected, rubbish-strewn ground, a couple of hours a week and virtually no money. I also had no plot security, as my Other Half pointed out whenever I suggested an investment such as a path ('It's not our plot' he would say), or a water butt ('not our plot') or a fence to stop the sweetcorn being blown flat ('not...' etc.). I read these books during my long commuting hours, resting my head against grimy train windows, trying to work out how I could use my few hours and fewer pennies to create a tidy oasis that would win medals for beauty and prizes for mammoth vegetables and feed my family with delicious meals that were sustainably grown and cooked with love. As time passed and I found ways to botch allotments into some semblance of neatness and productivity I've revisited those books with a more forgiving attitude: two or three favoured texts are now as close as friends, but I still had to filter their advice through the reality of working full-time and having a child, who, as he grew, was increasingly unwilling to spend all his free time on an allotment.

Although I didn't know it, I was being given a grounding in how to start a plot from scratch, and over the next decade I was to manage, co-work, or plot-sit eight different allotments, from the London fringes to Beachy Head. On each of them the issues were different but the problem was the same – how was this weedy/windy/waterlogged/parched/neglected/overworked bit of land to be made productive with not much time and almost no expenditure?

The books were great when it came to actually growing things, but almost useless on the subject of management. How do you take a summer break away from the plot when the six weeks of the school holiday are also the best weeks for harvesting what you've spent the other forty-six growing? What do you do with a glut? Which major investments are worth it and which are purely designed to separate the vulnerable grower from his or her cash? Above all, how does anybody with a job and/or family find enough time to run an allotment successfully?

We don't hear much about allotment guilt yet, but I suspect we will. The pale to mid greens who are the new generation of allotment-holders will be prone to it. The dark greens either got their allotment a decade ago, when the whole idea was still unfashionable, or are dedicated to growing alfalfa and sugar beets along disused railway lines or creating community gardens in car parks. They wouldn't feel guilt anyway, because their lives aren't about finding a balance between competing demands: they are green, they live green and everything else is secondary.

But for those who are still trying to reconcile food miles and trips to Pizza Express, or whose carbon footprint is challenged by their teenage offspring's daily devotion to hair straighteners that make the house lights dim whenever they are plugged in, allotment guilt will take its place in the ever-shuffling hand of responsibilities and burdens they have been dealt. This guilt is not just middle-class angst, a luxury of the under-busy; it's driven by local media attention which bellows about each sweet little old bloke or single mum whose allotment tenancy is terminated. A week later, the same journalist castigates 'the authorities' for the number of plots lying weedy and neglected despite the desperate growers begging for them, and claims it's a scandal to have decade-long allotment waiting lists, while land is snapped up by developers for supermarkets. All this makes the new allotment-holder scared and insecure before they've even got to grips with the complex idiosyncrasies and characteristics of the plot that they must – so swiftly – demonstrate is productive.

Learning your plot, then, means planting swift-growing crops as soon as you get your tenancy, and then spending as much time as possible doing things that will seem unproductive and lazy but will produce a dividend of good harvests a couple of years down the line.

The crops that sprint are also the ones that take most from the soil, so they are ideal to plant in containers filled with potting compost or a similar medium. These vegetables may be called 'catch crops' because canny allotment-holders plant them in between slower-growing ones and harvest them before the slower-growing crop gets into its stride. For a new allotment-holder, getting sprinter crops into containers or the soil can give a quick harvest, as well as the impression of productivity, and allow the new grower some time to learn the soil and weather conditions that make up the particular climate of their plot.

 ## Sprinter Crops

The summer radish is fastest out of the blocks, being harvestable in a month if conditions are perfect, but allow five weeks in a dull or rainy summer. Romping home soon after radishes are the dwarf French beans and lettuces, along with main crop peas, all of which produce a harvest within two or three months from planting. Spinach crosses the line at three months, along with kohlrabi and the smaller beetroot varieties (longer-rooted beets take another couple of weeks).

 ## Crops with Good Pace

Coming in between three and four months from planting to harvest are the climbing and runner beans (both of which require more comprehensive support structures than the dwarf French beans), calabrese (different varieties can be sown in spring or autumn, allowing those who get a plot later in the year to start sowing immediately), summer cabbage and salad onions (both of which will be ready to harvest around the four-month mark), and, coming in last, but very much not least, first early potatoes will take four months to produce a crop.

Green manures are also a great way to give your plot a boost while you get to learn its idiosyncrasies, and there are different manures for every time of year. A green manure is a crop that you sow from seed, and then dig into your soil to improve its quality – so it's like living compost. Most are fast-growing and you need to supervise them, as your neighbours will not thank you if the manure sets seed which colonises their beds. As your green manure starts to flower, cut off the flower heads to stop any seed setting (a nice sharp hoe allows you to do this without straining your back, if you don't own a scythe) and leave the crop on the soil surface for a few days to soften. Then simply dig it into the soil.

Winter Green Manures

- Plant rye between August (in the north of the UK) and October (southern counties) and leave over the winter – it's a great crop for making an insulating blanket that keeps nutrients in and soil warm. Don't let the seed drift into cultivated areas though, as it can be a swine to weed out from between other plants.

- Field beans can be planted between September and November and fix a lot of nitrogen in exhausted soils. They are extremely hardy but don't provide such good ground cover.

Summer Green Manures

Crimson clover is a sprinter that produces lots of lovely red flowers, popular with bees and not a worry to your neighbours as it's not a seed that travels easily. Sow from April to September but expect to dig in around December as it really doesn't cope well with winter, especially if your soil is heavy. Cutting the flowering heads off can produce a second crop, if you don't dig in within a week or so.

Mustard provides a bulky, fibrous top growth that can be incorporated into the soil either by digging in or by worms. If it dies in a hard frost, simply let it lie on the ground where it will provide a mulch and slowly be taken down into the soil by worms and weather action. Whatever is left can be dug in during your spring working of the soil. If you have a really sandy allotment, you can leave your mustard to get to around forty centimetres so that it improves your soil condition even more, but most people will chop it down and dig it in after around two months. Mustard is also the green manure of choice if you have wireworms or eelworms hollowing out your potatoes. Wireworms feed ravenously on a dug-in mustard crop and as a result they mature quickly and fly off as click beetles to lay eggs in grassland, so as long as you keep your plot dug over (and don't have grass paths) the cultivated land should be clear for potatoes within a year. Eelworms, on the other hand, are tiny creatures that are laid in cysts. I'm told that growing mustard causes them to hatch before there is anything for them to eat so they die.

One of the more disturbing things about allotment life, apart from a delight in digging and a tendency to hand bagfuls of glutting crops to complete strangers, is the relish that most allotment-holders take in learning about the life (and death) cycles of pests. One of the first people we met when we were given 'not' our plot was Maisie, a woman whose soft-heartedness in most respects was legendary. She had once left her allotment hat hanging up in her shed for the entire winter because an orb spider had laid an egg sac in it and she didn't want to disturb the babies. As Maisie was also the kind of woman who had a demanding coiffure that involved monthly blonde highlights plus a weekly shampoo and set, this was a considerable sacrifice. She also fed the foxes that lived on the site, provided fat-balls for winter birds and objected to slug pellets as being cruel and unnecessary.

Maisie was generously built and favoured bright floral tops which could lead to confusion in the bumble bee population: it wasn't unusual to see her standing stock still on her plot, reasoning with a bee that was trying to extract pollen from one of the flowers on her T-shirt. She was the only allotment-holder I knew who matched her nail varnish to her allotment tools, favouring a salmon pink in summer that toned with her 'lady's' fork and trowel set and a deep chestnut colour in winter to tone with her designer wellington boots.

For all her love of comfort and generous nature, Maisie loathed caterpillars and telephoned me one day to say that she'd seen a documentary on a nature channel about wasps that laid eggs in caterpillars. She knew that I'd 'been abroad a lot', as she put it, and wondered if I could 'get somebody to bring' her some of those wasps. It wasn't easy to explain that wildlife trafficking was an offence, and for several weeks she pursued me around the site, trying to persuade me that a few wasps transported in a tobacco tin wouldn't cause any problems. Eventually she let go of the subject, but continued to seek out ways to wreak havoc on the cabbage white population and constantly regaled me with new facts relating to caterpillar predators and how she intended to encourage them. From April to late July her allotment took on a Miss Havisham appearance, as every bed and border was festooned with old net curtains which Maisie used as caterpillar netting, and if Maisie herself hadn't been as blonde and curvy as Mae West, the plot could have been unpleasantly eerie.

Maisie was not alone. One allotment-holder I knew in London used to 'fire-bomb' slugs with a blowtorch; another had the habit of hiding mousetraps in her shed, to the fury of her husband who more than once had them snap his (fortunately gloved) fingers when reaching for tools on a dark shelf. His wife refused to use humane mousetraps on the basis that 'she wanted the little buggers good and dead': their plot had a particular problem with rodents eating pea seedlings, but such bloodthirstiness suggested a bit of a Lady Macbeth complex in the making, and we all felt a little sorry for both the mice and the man.

Winter Necessities

If you're a relatively new allotment-holder, you might be thinking that there's little or nothing to do on your plot in November and December. Not so. This is the time of year to make investments for the future, both horticulturally and socially.

Digging is a task that you should launch into now, and continue with whenever the soil allows. Normally, if you've taken over a neglected plot, you'll have done some surface work through the summer to be able to grow plants, but the real work, the literal below-the-surface work, is done through the winter.

For soil to be vital and fecund, it needs to be aerated, friable and full of organic matter. Aerating is the first purpose of digging: working the ground with a fork involves breaking up the compacted surface, tearing apart the roots of grass and perennial weeds and removing them, and shattering clumps of soil that have become so solid that water cannot penetrate them. This alone improves the ground's productivity because air and water continue the process of separating soil grains, especially through freezing which blasts tiny soil particles apart as water droplets expand into ice.

Making soil friable allows one fragment of earth to move against another. This lets more air and water penetrate and encourages the separation of the surface and also makes it easier for plants, especially seedlings, to get their roots moving out and down easily. It's roughly analogous to the difference between pushing your hand into an open bag of feathers (friable earth) or attempting the same with a feather cushion (compacted soil) – your hand will reach the bottom of the bag within moments, but will be pushed back by the cover that surrounds the cushion. You need to dig your ground, increasing its friability, to give your crops a fighting chance.

Digging is tough, but digging which incorporates some organic matter is much easier because with each forkful that you turn over, you immediately add into the soil mix something that loosens the soil and, if it's clay-based, stops it sticking back together again. If you have a sandy soil, this organic addition is just as necessary, as sandy soils lose nutrients like kids lose letters home from school! So digging in compost or manure adds organic value to your earth, whatever its original nature, and makes your life easier for years ahead.

Whenever it's not too wet or too frozen, you need to be digging. Too wet is when the soil sticks together and compacts under your feet – all you're doing if you turn over sodden earth is encouraging it to stick together even more. And when it's frozen, you can't dig, because the fork or spade bounces back into your hand as if you'd hit rock. There are good social reasons to dig too, because this is the time when the old guard start casting a bitter eye on their 'summer' neighbours. It's a fact that around a third of allotment-holders who join our site are never seen from November to April, and while that could be considered their choice and their business, waiting lists are filling up with people who want a plot. This means many plots remain unused right through the winter, to the fury of all those who wander round allotments (and I used to be one of them) making acid comments about the way the place looks more like waste ground, and how much more effective they would be if they were ever lucky enough to reach the top of the list and get a plot of their own.

It's not the fair-weather allotment-holder who bears the brunt of this ill-tempered commentary – it's the all-year-round grower, whose blameless good behaviour leaves him or her trying to explain the situation. So if you're a summer-only allotment grower, be prepared for some sarcastic asides from your neighbours who've been apologising for you all winter!

It's not difficult to improve your plot's productivity and to continue to grow delicious vegetables right through the winter, but it does require a bit more organisation than summer visits to the plot. First, make sure you're properly equipped. You need hard-soled boots to dig properly, or you will cripple your feet for weeks. Take a flask of hot drink, or have a gas or storm kettle to make something warming while you're on the plot, as you often don't notice how long you've been working in the cold until you stop and find you're shivering and tired. Carry a torch as evenings arrive quickly and few sites have lighting: trudging back to the gate in slippery muddy boots, along dark paths, when you're knackered is one of the most dispiriting and spooky experiences available to allotment-holders, and it's completely avoidable!

Take a whistle if you're going to be working alone. Of course nothing bad will happen to you, because it doesn't happen to the vast majority of allotment-holders, but if you are unlucky enough to be one of the tiny minority, allotment sites are big and dark, and there may not be anybody nearby to hear you call out. The sound of a whistle travels a lot further and is less exhausting than shouting out loud. I've heard of allotment-holders who've dislocated hips by slipping on wet paths, or trodden on rusty nails and been unable to walk, and even one who got locked in her own shed by her husband who was listening to his iPod and failed to hear her shout of alarm. A whistle is tiny, but it can really be a life-saver.

Early winter is a time when actually getting to work on the allotment can be a rare event, even for the most enthusiastic – frosts in the North and rains everywhere, plus the risk of fog, mist, hail and gales, depending on geographic location, make this one of the most unpredictable and difficult months, plant-wise. But it's also one of the most rewarding periods for the committed allotment-grower.

Apart from the digging, which becomes a masochistic pleasure of quite disturbing proportions, there's the solitude. You may not see anybody else on the site all day, if you're lucky enough to get up there for a whole day, but you'll probably find yourself being scrutinised by a range of allotment wildlife that seems to consider winter visitors as free entertainment. Robins hog the soil as you turn it over, grabbing worms, and you'll be observed by allotment foxes, many of whom have given up their nocturnal lifestyle in favour of lounging around in disused compost bins, waiting to see what the visitors will leave behind in the way of leek roots, windfall fruit and – with any luck – some sandwich crusts. On our site I only ever see jays between November and December, when they scold the foxes for nicking rotten fruit and raise their crests at me as I trudge to and fro with my fork.

Silence is a rare experience in the modern world, but the silence of an allotment is a special one – it's not the carefully marshalled calm of a half-hour in a meditation room: it's full of tiny non-silences that make it, somehow, even more quiet. Quarrelling birds have the odd Jerry Springer moment, avian-style, and leave behind them a noiselessness that is even more relaxing. There are occasional worrying sounds: tiny scurries and susurrations that suggest your plot may be hosting mice, or even rats, although the noises could just be dried leaves rustling in the corners. The thunk of the fork or spade in the soil and the granular whisper of the earth being turned make a rhythm with your own (often laboured) breathing that becomes almost symphonic and can lead you to complete a few more rows of digging than you'd intended, to the detriment of your aching back later in the day. Digging, in fact, becomes its own purpose, and why you are digging fades completely from your mind as you focus on the pleasure of the activity and the way your attention narrows to the unturned earth in front of you, and your effect upon it.

Digging isn't just about soil preparation, though: the sound of a parsnip or leek coming free from the soil is like a minuscule avalanche, and, particularly with parsnips, if you've already spent a good few minutes digging them out, you concentrate hard on what you can hear, for fear of missing the tiny cracking sound that could mean you haven't dug far enough (although it feels like you're halfway to China) and your magnificent long root has begun to snap. The warning creak is enough to tell you that you need to let go of the leaves and get your trowel or fork back into the earth, excavating even further around the vegetable so as to stop it breaking and leaving its pointed extremity in the ground.

You get to see your plot at its worst in winter. Among other things, you'll discover where standing water makes puddles that will drown anything planted there; if the path harbours treacherous moss or lichen to cause you to perform one of those slapstick pratfalls that are simply hilarious to everybody except you, the comedian with a plate-sized bruise on your backside for the next three weeks; which surrounding trees dump leaves on your soil, requiring you to rake them up, dry them and burn them, because they might harbour diseases if you put them in the compost. It's like seeing a new lover when they are ill – it tells you the worst that you can expect in future and gives you a chance to prepare yourself for it. A lover may not be a project, but an allotment certainly is, and improving the drainage, raising the path and getting the tree pruned are all activities that make the years ahead much more of a pleasure and less of a pain – particularly for your rear end!

The other rewards are purely hedonistic: the first Brussels sprouts, as tiny and hard as chestnuts, ideal blanched and served with brie and bacon; or leaves of kale, deep green and tightly crinkled and perfect for stir-fries with oyster mushrooms and garlic; leeks which are more juicy and eye-watering by far than the mild papery objects you buy in supermarkets; and those parsnips, the ones you worked so hard to dig up, as heavy as elephant tusks but sweet-smelling and draped with whiskery roots like an Oriental grandfather's beard.

When you take your winter haul home, you feel virtuous and frugal, and when you eat it, and discover the extra taste and texture that you get from fresh winter veg, you're reminded that while anybody can harvest a few lettuces in summer, it takes a real grower to produce good winter vegetables.

It's common for people to have an aversion to kale, and the way to overcome it is to feed them Kale Luxury – a stir-fried recipe that links a winter vegetable to summery flavours and removes all the nasty elements of 'eating your greens'.

Because the kale isn't cooked in water it doesn't become slimy or give off the aroma that so many of us associate with unappetising messes of green bitterness that we were forced to eat before we could have our puddings. In fact, the orange butter sauce is a bit like having your pudding with your kale, and the citrus flavour, combined with the nutty sesame seeds, is a million miles from childhood memories of glum winter dinners.

KALE LUXURY

INGREDIENTS

• A good haul of very small kale leaves (take a few from each plant), washed well to remove grit and with the ribs torn out

• Sunflower oil and toasted sesame oil

• 1 clove garlic, minced

• 1 large orange (the cheap marmalade oranges from the supermarket are fine for this), zested and juiced

• A small handful of sesame seeds

• 1 tablespoon salted butter

• Black, or black and pink, peppercorns

METHOD

Shake the kale well in a colander to remove as much water as possible.

Put a wok or large frying pan over a medium heat and pour in a teaspoon of sunflower oil. Add the garlic and cook, stirring, until just becoming golden. Throw in the kale and stir well, ensuring that the kale wilts down and becomes dark green, almost black, and has a soft clinging movement as you turn it over in the pan rather than a springy resistant one.

Add the orange zest and take a moment to breathe in the glorious scent produced: the aroma of citrus on top of very fresh kale is a bit like drinking a Mai Tai on a salty beach!

When the kale is fully wilted, but before the garlic becomes too dark in colour (which would give a bitter flavour), turn down the heat just a little and add the sesame seeds to toast them slightly – you aren't trying to make them golden, simply to warm them enough to release their flavour.

Make a little well in the middle of the greens and pour the orange juice and a teaspoon of toasted sesame oil into it. Plop the butter into the middle of that puddle and begin to turn the kale over into it, so that as the butter melts, all the kale becomes coated in a rich buttery sauce. This only takes a few seconds.

To serve, place on warm plates and grind pepper over the top.

Delicious with pork or lamb, this is also a lovely accompaniment to gnocchi or egg noodles for a quick but nutritious lunch.

Does My Plot Look Big in This?

There's a certain minimum without which you cannot manage an allotment – not even a quarter plot – and the investment needs to be made within a few months of getting your plot. For the first weeks, maybe even months, you can manage by transporting all your gardening equipment from home, but once you decide to commit to your plot for the long term, it becomes easier to have tools on-site, as long as your site allows it. Sites vary immensely: some allow sheds, some only allow lockboxes and some don't even permit that. There are sites with communal storage and sites with lockers – I even know one site with showers! Generally though, the shed is the classic route to keeping things together on the plot.

I'd say that your absolute capsule wardrobe of tools, kit and clothing is:

- Spade and fork
- Rake
- Hoe

- Trowel

- Pruners

- Shears (if you have grass paths)

- Canes

- String and penknife

- Wheelbarrow (or two big buckets)

- Hosepipe (or two big watering cans)

- Labels (posh copper ones look impressive if you're rich, cheap plastic ones work just as well if you're not)

- Wellingtons or hiking boots (I prefer hiking boots but wellingtons are the standard garb)

- Jeans you don't mind destroying

- Waterproof jacket

- Cap (a winter hat is nice too, but a cap is the year-round classic: flat, tweed or baseball according to your age and preference!)

- Robust gloves

- Kneeler pad

- Torch and whistle if you're working alone

This list won't make your allotment life exactly easy, but it will make it possible to work your plot for a couple of months while you decide if you want to commit to a future of growing your own.

If you're allowed a shed, a good sturdy padlock is essential. Depending on security on-site, it may be better not to store expensive items in your shed, but as many people don't have anywhere at home to store bulky items like strimmers or rotovators, you may have no choice but to leave them on the plot. I think that if you have nothing of great value to steal, you should leave a window uncovered so that the opportunistic thief can see you're not worth the trouble and move on, but if you do have equipment that has a resale value, put plywood covers over the inside of your windows or, even better, use scrap decking so that it looks as if you've made it really difficult for anybody to get in. We hang wooden window covers from large hooks so that we can take them down when we're on-site but it looks as if the windows are boarded up from the outside when we leave.

Most thieves target allotment sites after dark, so having windows that look difficult to break, and a padlock and sturdy door that suggest your shed is going to be a tough target, can be all that's necessary to get them to try a less well-defended plot. Of course this only moves the problem to your neighbours, but if everybody gets better at protecting allotment property and possessions, it helps prevent the incursions made by thieves who are often badly-organised hooligans rather than career criminals, and therefore can be dissuaded from their behaviour if the effort becomes too great for the reward they obtain.

Allotment theft is like allotment guilt – hardly discussed but distressing to those experiencing it. Losing treasured equipment is horrible, having your shed broken into feels like a violation and if your crops are taken or trashed too, it can begin to feel as if your life, as well as your property, is being destroyed. Some councils are great about security – the site on which 'not' our plot is located has excellent fences and gates – but others are downright dismissive of the need to help tenants protect their crops, and choose not to support allotment-holders in creating a healthy lifestyle on a safe site. The police, in my experience, are supportive but unable to do much to help allotment-holders. Building a sense of community, good security habits and establishing contacts with the local press can all help allotment sites that feel besieged by vandals or petty thieves to turn the situation around – local councils don't like bad publicity and local papers love to cover community stories, so a run of bad press can often persuade a council to invest in support for allotment-holders.

Back to tools and kit – at the other end of the spectrum from allotment minimalism is the *Top Gear* school of equipment purchase whose adherents know the performance of every petrol-driven power tool on the market. Those who belong to this fraternity are usually male, often in a second marriage – possibly because their first wife became new-technology-intolerant – and have an allotment that is flatter, finer-soiled and more weed-free than any other. They don't necessarily have crops, and any tree or shrub has been pruned to within (or past) an inch of its life, but their plots are always tidy. The *Top Gear* guys also tend to have an extremely robust shed with the kind of lock that even a sonic screwdriver would struggle to open.

My favourite man in this group is Ted, who is so dedicated to his vast range of complex gardening machinery that he is willing to travel across three counties to put in several hours' hard labour on somebody else's allotment just to demonstrate the superiority of his rotovator, strimmer, chainsaw, mulcher or leaf-blower. I love Ted dearly and hope he never reads this book and works out that he is single-handedly doing equipment hire companies out of a large amount of business in the south of England! He has been one of the first visitors to almost every plot on which I've worked, and his enthusiasm to demonstrate his latest bit of kit has regularly saved me weeks of hard labour. Ted's wife Chloe (his second wife, please note) is understanding of his petrol-driven mania – she sometimes calls me when she's planning a shopping trip to ask if I'd like to borrow him for the day so that she can spend the whole day browsing the boutiques, confident that Ted is happily ripping something up, down or out with his noisy, smelly, beloved machines.

But that's the point: if you really must rotovate – and it can be necessary (I've done it myself), but it's like root canal work, expensive, exhausting and sometimes more painful than the problem it's meant to address – why not see if you can hire the beastly machine? Ditto everything else on the jobs-you-do-once-a-year list. Find three or four other allotment-holders to chip in for a weekend's hire so that you can get several plots done and divide the price between you.

Most plot-holders fall somewhere between the extremes of parsimony and total machine pride and add a few items to our list of necessities such as:

- Trug

- Pest-control sprayer (even if it's just soapy water)

- Pots and seed trays

- Maximum and minimum thermometer

- Compost bin (if your local council offers cheap bins it can be better to buy one than try constructing your own, at least for the first couple of years)

Each individual has their own bottom line when it comes to kitting out their plot, and finding out what you can't live without can be a lifelong process, during which you tend to accumulate quite a lot of items that you used once and didn't get on with – those bits of equipment then sidle to the back of the shed, looking dusty and apologetic and not quite sure whether they are welcome. In Barnes they used to hold a bring-and-buy day on one allotment site, where you could offload your unwanted strimmer or aerator and pick up a good folding wheelbarrow or propagator to replace it, but most of the time you and your unloved machinery have to settle for an ill-tempered truce in which you mutter whenever you see the offending article and the article retaliates by snagging bits of netting or string around itself whenever you want said netting or string in a screaming hurry.

The issue of capital expenditure on 'not' our plot was coming to a head for me and OH and it wasn't the foamy, delicious head of a pint of beer after several hours of hard labour on the plot. This was the rank, slow-bubbling head that sometimes forms on comfrey soup if the weather gets too hot before you manage to pour it into your potato trenches. The issue was, as so often between us, water.

I wanted another water butt, in advance of an expected hosepipe ban. OH thought this unnecessary, and would continue to do so, right up to the day when the ban was in place, at which point he would become as bad-tempered as a rudely woken bear whenever we had to go and water: in other words, every other day. For the sake of my mental health and our marriage I was determined to win the battle: not least because I'd already bought the water butt and hidden it behind the shed where the council staff kept their tools.

I'd decided that an oblique approach was best, so I was enlisting fellow water-conservation enthusiasts to fight on my behalf. Celia had given us an excellent lecture on the relationship between hard tap water and potato scab which she later told me she'd made up on the spot, and which left OH quietly mulling all day. Chaz was primed with an account of how allotment thieves targeted those with hosepipes and I knew that his immoral authority, as a man who'd learned to garden in borstal, would have a profound effect.

I was waiting for Maisie to come past, so I could tell her it was time for her contribution, when I saw HSM in the distance, at which point overconfidence caused me to wave her and her brood over.

HSM stood for Home-Schooling Mother and I wanted to like her, I really did, but... As an example, HSM's three children spent a lot of time at the allotment. There was no reason why they shouldn't, as long as they were also learning whatever lessons were appropriate, but something about the way they walked – in single file, their heads down, the little boy kicking at tussocks of grass while his sisters trailed hand tools behind them as they dawdled – suggested they regarded the hours spent on their plot as penitential.

HSM objected to man-made fibres so her offspring wore cotton or wool. Possibly her objections extended to synthetic dyes, as their clothes were not only natural fabrics, but in colours that implied an arcane boiling up of nettle and walnut, possibly in a dank glade where savage rites took place at dark of moon. The kids looked like object lessons in Dickensian misery but decked out in medieval garb. It was a good thing they didn't go to school because their peculiar grey and brown garments, complete with sagging hems, would have caused them to be mocked and become even more miserable than they appeared to be when they were on-site.

HSM was a paragon of self-sufficiency, which is why I wanted to like her. She baked her own bread and was trying to cultivate her own grain. She spun wool. She knew the common name of every native plant and enough botanical ones to give my horticulturally-replete friend Celia a run for her money. HSM was hard-working and resourceful and utterly insufferable. She'd upset the committee by telling them that making a profit from the allotment shop was wrong, even though the profit was immediately ploughed back into improving the site. Her loud and regularly repeated opinions included the claim that Chaz was an environmental despoiler because he owned a petrol-driven chainsaw, and that parents who sent their children to the local secondary school were handing innocence over to Mammon and sin – this seemed mainly to be based on the fact that there was a tuck shop that sold sweets to raise funds for the school library. Even Maisie, who normally saved all her negativity for her allotment neighbour Felix, had once said that HSM could spoil a good day just by turning up.

Already I was regretting my rashness but it was too late: HSM stood before me, her three children behind her like drab toys whose clockwork mechanisms had run down simultaneously. Early in my time on the site, I had offered them cake. Cake, HSM said, was poison. I did take offence at that, especially as the cake in question was a particularly good blackberry crumble-cake with hedgerow blackberries, which I had thought she'd rather approve of, as she was a keen forager. The little boy, Ayar, had actually bitten my finger in his eagerness to commit death-by-baking before his mother could stop him, and an uneasy truce was now maintained by dint of the little ones remaining outside my plot's fence on their mother's instructions, presumably in case I tempted them into my gingerbread shed and threw them in the oven.

As I say, I tried extremely hard to like HSM but had never yet succeeded. I waved at the children and the two girls smiled back uncertainly, but Ayar just stared at me with tragic eyes and bit his fingernails.

After a few awkward words on the weather, she strode off, the children moping behind her, and I wondered once again what their home life was like. I had a mental image of unsprung mattresses and gruel consumed by candlelight and went off to talk to Celia to remove it from my imagination.

Celia was cathartic, as usual, but left me feeling inadequate. She was planting blue potatoes and harvesting seed from her Sutherland kale, a rare variety whose seed bank she was single-handedly restocking. There were days when I wondered how you became a Celia: was something sprinkled on you at birth, like Fairy Growmore, or did you receive a series of horticultural lucky breaks that led to you being able to grow plants that other people couldn't even pronounce?

When I got back to 'Nearly' our plot, OH had arrived and was talking to Felix. This was not good news. Felix and

Maisie's feud was epic: for many years they had been on opposite sides of the (literal) fence on any issue and in enlisting Maisie I had necessarily had to leave Felix out of the water butt conspiracy. As if by malign intuition he was offering OH exactly the opposite opinion to the one that Maisie had been primed to issue.

'Felix reckons we'd be wasting our money on another water butt,' said OH.

I glared at Felix, aware that if I lost the argument, the money on the water butt would definitely be wasted, and he smiled back, happily unaware that he was destroying my dreams. There was something very wholesome-looking about Felix, who was ruddy and broad-shouldered with twinkling blue eyes and who spoke slowly with a rolling local accent that had all but disappeared from Brighton and Hove, being heard only in the remoter villages of Sussex. He had enormous hands, scarred from years of hard manual labour, and the kind of outdoor tan that comes from constant work in the fresh air rather than from a couple of weeks' holiday in the sun. If you had to pick the most trustworthy-looking son-of-the-soil from the entire allotment roster you'd almost certainly pick Felix, which would be a mistake, as he was definitely the shadiest member of our community and always had a crafty scheme percolating somewhere in the recesses of his devious brain.

'And anyway,' OH added, with the absolute finality that I knew from long experience, 'we have to remember that it's not our plot.'

The hosepipe ban was imposed within a fortnight, and OH expressed his views on trudging to and fro with watering cans each time we went to the plot. I thought about raising the water butt issue again, but my pride wouldn't allow me to admit that I'd tried and failed to trick him. The water butt lurked behind the council tool shed for several weeks before I managed to sell it to some new allotment-holders for about half what I'd paid for it. Every time I entered the 'not our plot' shed I glared at the 'essential' leaf-blower we'd only used once and the 'got to have it' long-handled hoe that I couldn't lift and OH never bothered with because he could hand-weed almost every inch of the plot, and wished I'd just paid Chaz to put the damn water butt up for me.

It goes to prove that accessorising your plot is almost a compulsion and certain items become addictive. I have a thing about trugs, and Celia is the owner of more trowels than one woman could use in a lifetime – she is an Imelda Marcos of trowels, right down to keeping them in boxes in her wardrobe. Seeds, of course, are the easiest allotment item on which to overspend, and no matter how often I suggest to people that they pal up with a neighbour and buy seeds together, most people still come into our shop every week and wander out with two or three packets of seed, each of which contains enough seed to fill an entire ten-rod plot.

After seed, compulsive spending tends to kick in around the hand tools: secateurs, hand forks, trowels and dibbers are priced at a level that always make you feel you're getting a bargain, and are seductively marketed to suggest that each new form or style fulfils a need you didn't know, until then, you had. They are also the easiest bits of kit to lose on the plot, or leave at home if you don't have a shed, necessitating the borrowing or buying of a new item or a return home to locate the one you've forgotten. As there's nearly always a hardware store or garden centre within easy distance of an allotment site, many folk will nip down and buy a cheap set of hand tools, only to find the trowel bends like toffee when confronted with anything tougher than dry sand and the fork immediately prongs itself on a stone and refuses to have the tines straightened again, necessitating the purchase of a better, more heavy-duty set next time you go shopping – only to lose that one too...

The answer to the loss of hand tools is simple – and it's why I have so many trugs. Never move a step on your plot without taking your trug or basket or even one of those rubber buckets that garden centres sell. If you are using a soft plastic bucket, don't rely on the small, palm-lacerating handles; instead, loop a good wide strap or old belt through the handles and use this to sling the bucket over your shoulder as you move around the plot.

Whatever your chosen receptacle, put your hand tools in it and train yourself to never put them anywhere but back in their carrier. It takes about a month to learn to always replace items where you took them from, but it saves you a fortune.

I can't recommend the clever belts and aprons that are offered for sale in upmarket gardening magazines, because I've found that they tend to pick up mud and water by capillary action every time you bend over or kneel down. After a couple of hours, my aprons always end up like small mud huts with feet underneath! Perhaps neater cultivators than me can make this system work, but I've never seen an allotment-holder wearing a tool belt or an apron, so I suspect my experience is not unique.

Melon-Growing Secrets

I was having a moment of social paranoia, usually an almost impossible allotment experience, and my Other Half was unsympathetic. The problem was Errol and Bert, or should it be Errol (comma) and Bert?

'Who cares?' said OH.

Well, I did. Errol and Bert had back-to-back allotments, or one big allotment, depending on how you looked at things. Errol and Bert shared a house, or Bert had Errol as a lodger, depending on how you looked at things. They were a couple, or they were two old codgers thrown together by life – depending on how you looked at things.

Bert grew the best (in some years the only) watermelons on this windy south coast allotment site. Errol was born in New Zealand and named after the actor from the same part of the world. Bert and Errol were both in their seventies but evaded questions about their exact ages.

'I think that's indicative,' I said. OH ignored me. 'Well, I think gay men are a bit more coy about revealing their age, don't you?'

OH's studied silence told me I was either generalising wildly and offensively, or boring him, or possibly both. But it did matter. Errol and Bert had every right to keep their personal life (or lives) private, but in the past few weeks, Bert's plot, never exactly tidy, had become downright unkempt. He'd been sent a weed notice, the allotment equivalent of a yellow card, by the council, which he had not commented on in public, nor responded to in any horticulturally appropriate way. So the question troubling me was not prurient but practical – if they were a couple, Errol could be asked to take over the tenancy of Bert's plot and bring it up to his own meticulous standards. But if not, Bert was facing a thirty-day eviction notice at the next committee meeting – and while we all liked him, and he'd been an allotment-holder longer than some of us had been alive, we couldn't play favourites. Bert's only other known relative was a daughter who lived in London – she wasn't close enough to take over her father's plot, even if she wanted to.

'You're thinking about the daughter, aren't you?' I asked OH. 'It's true that having a daughter does seem to suggest that Bert isn't gay. But, according to Maisie, Bert's wife left him and moved back in with her own parents before the little girl was two. It was a local scandal at the time, apparently. So that actually backs up my assertion in a way – if Bert was homosexual and married to try and conceal it, well…'

I waved my arms, indicating the general social repression of same sex relationships half a century ago. OH finally looked up from the beans he was hoeing.

'Which one's Bert?' he asked.

I sighed. The two men were hardly indistinguishable: Bert was tall and bald and dressed like a tramp while Errol was small and neat, with slicked-back dark hair that had only just started to grey. But OH, like many allotment-holders, knew people by their crops rather than any other indicator.

'Bert the watermelons,' I replied.

'Ah.' Long silence, punctuated by the sound of the hoe hitting pebbles. 'I do wonder...'

'Yes?' At last, some concern!

'How does he grow them when nobody else can?'

I left him to hoe and went to talk to Maisie.

One of the almost unnoticed changes in recent years has been the number of women taking on allotments, or keeping them on when their husbands pass away. Two decades ago, when I visited my first allotment site in London, the allotment-holders were probably ninety per cent male. Women appeared on the site only to cut flowers, or pick fruit, or if 'the old man' was ill, when they would be sent up to deputise. The site had fifty plots and only two were being cultivated by women. Today, at least in the south of England, nearly half the plots are registered to women.

Maisie was one of the early pioneers. Her brother had been at school with Bert and she remembered him and Bert hiding apples in her pram when they were nearly caught scrumping. She'd taken over her father's allotment when he had a stroke, 'just for a few weeks, until the family decided what to do'. By the time he died, three years later, she had become an expert grower. She'd been running the plot for over three decades when I met her, harvesting plums from a tree her father had grown from a pit he found in a pot of jam he'd bought at a fête in the 1950s and supplying knowledge of local growing conditions, families and shop bargains with equal accuracy.

Even so, I couldn't ask Maisie if Bert was gay: it would have been trespassing on the unwritten rules that governed life for the 'old school' allotment-holders, who almost never brought their personal lives to the plot, unlike the younger generation, who often seemed to view the role of horticulture as a form of therapy, and happily expounded on their addictions, failed romances and other problems at a volume that could even be heard above petrol mowers and strimmers.

Anyway, it wasn't so much Maisie's input I needed as her winning ways with Rosa, Bert's dog, a large, hostile, cross-greyhound-Alsatian with an amazing turn of speed for a twelve-year-old. If she didn't manage to nip you before you knew she was there, she would fall back on an incessant low growl and I believed she could throw her voice because several times when I was sure she'd been threatening away on one side of me, she'd appeared on the other side at the same moment and tried to bite me.

As Rosa never actually left Bert's plot to pursue a victim, you were pretty safe unless you opened his gate, in which case you needed swift reflexes and nerves of steel... or Maisie. She wasn't so much a dog whisperer as a dog threatener and it began as soon as she put her hand on the latch, 'Come on then, Rosa, you bitch. Let's see you try your nasty ways on me. I'll give you a taste of your own medicine if you dare to tackle me, you wicked old cow...', etc., all the way up the front path. Rosa had respect for Maisie and homicidal intent for everybody else, so Maisie was often called on to be a minder for the site reps as they toured the plots, checking everybody was keeping to a fair level of cultivation.

Bert got to his plot just after dawn and left around two. Errol arrived around noon and left around sunset, so between them they had the daylight hours covered. They had a set of rules governing plot maintenance too: each would water for the other, but not harvest or weed. Manure spreading and bonfires were always joint affairs and they combined their efforts to harvest the greengages from the tree on the boundary between their plots, often giving the gages to HSM who paid them back with a couple of jars of the jam she made from the fruit.

Bert never touched Errol's prize (literally) chrysanthemums and Errol was banned from approaching Bert's watermelon beds. In fact, everybody was banned, and I had once expressed my idle suspicion that Bert only pretended to grow watermelons and actually purchased them from Waitrose, smuggling them in at sunrise when nobody was around to spot him. That earned me six weeks of silent treatment from Bert and had taught me not to share my other belief that Rosa's primary function was to scare away any nosy growers keen to discover the melon cultivation secrets Bert refused to divulge.

When we got to the twin plots, Bert was nowhere to be seen. Errol was, however, with Rosa lurking behind him like an elderly, hairy, ballistic missile programmed for one last act of eccentric damage, but for once he was as uncommunicative as his partner (or landlord) and offered no explanation for Bert's absence, nor any suggestion that he knew about the weed notice and was going to tackle the issue, or Bert, or both. His dry sense of humour was absent, which felt almost like an emotional amputation. Errol was legendary for the aridity of his wit – my favourite example was the young allotment-holder who turned up on-site one morning with a carrier bag bulging with citrus fruit and a glass lemon squeezer.

'Errol told me I needed to lime my plot,' he said.

'Are you sure that's what he meant?' I peered into the bag which was indeed full of limes.

'Yeah, he told me everybody does it, but that if you want to be organic you can't buy that powdered lime stuff, you have to make it yourself.'

I left him to it, and never explained why he had so many visitors that day, nor why everybody was in such a good mood as they watched him squeeze his limes and sprinkle the juice on what he was confident would be the best broccoli bed on the site.

Now Errol was morose, I was unhappy about the situation, and Maisie's well-meaning blather about the intimate details of a feud between two allotment-holders over a lost watering can did not distract me. In three weeks' time, Bert was likely to lose his allotment.

For the next couple of days, I found myself haunting Bert and Errol's area of the site, and avoiding my committee colleagues in case they wanted to talk about the situation. Bert was definitely there one day, but lurked in his shed with Rosa across the threshold like a territorial doormat, and the other days he wasn't there, which was downright unnerving. Errol turned up every afternoon and was evasive about Bert.

'I asked him what was going on and he looked very… twitchy,' I said to OH.

'Ask him what Bert does to those watermelons and watch him twitch then,' said OH, bitterly. He was looking at a row of caterpillar-nibbled spring cabbages, which explained some of his bitterness.

I lied at the committee meeting. I said Bert was ill. That sneaky claim has haunted me ever since. It bought Bert and Errol, or Bert (comma) and Errol, a two-month reprieve but when I went down to tell Bert, he wasn't there. Again.

I hung around until Errol turned up, with Rosa fulminating behind him on the end of an extremely robust lead.

'Thanks, love,' he said, when I explained what I'd done. 'But it's not necessary. Bert's gone.'

I stared at him, thinking the worst had happened, but actually it was worse than I'd thought: Bert wasn't dead – he had been taken away.

'Some bloody nosy neighbour rang that daughter,' Errol said. 'She came down and took one look and now he's in her house in Croydon. They're going to put him in a home.'

'Why?'

'She says he's senile.' Errol looked at Rosa. 'Well, he is, to be fair. Doesn't know anything or anybody these days, except the bloody dog. It's been weeks since he recognised me.'

There was a long silence in which I wondered what to say next. In a way, I knew Bert and Errol pretty well, but in another way we were almost strangers – I'd never been to their house, had no idea what they did when they weren't growing things, and didn't even know their surnames.

Errol shrugged. 'I've got to admit it was getting to be a strain. He tried to brain me with a saucepan last week when I came back from the plot and he thought I was a burglar. If Rosa hadn't wagged her tail I think he might never have believed I lived there. Anyway, that daughter of his whipped him off double-quick. You'd have thought I was the one doing the braining.'

'So what happens now?' I asked.

Errol looked at Rosa again, and she looked at me and I realised that nothing was going to happen and Bert was gone for good.

Two weeks later, Errol wrote to the committee and said that his allotment and Bert's would both be vacated by the end of the month for reallocation. I kept trying to find him up on his plot, but he was never around when I was, or if he was, he hid in the shed and I was too scared to approach with Rosa the random biter on the loose.

On the last day of Errol's tenancy, he turned up on the plot I was caretaking, with Rosa on the lead again, and a small, much-folded envelope in his hand.

'This is for you,' he said.

I took it gingerly, Rosa's hatred rising to a shrill warble as my hand touched Errol's, before subsiding again to a low growl.

'So what are you going to do now?' I asked.

'We're moving to Bridlington,' Errol indicated Rosa with his thumb. 'I'm getting a mobile home up there.'

'But...'

Errol looked away. 'I went to see Bert last week in the home that daughter's found for him. He was still in his pyjamas, sat watching TV with other old folk. Never even knew I was there. I'm going to Bridlington and that's that.'

I nodded and he plodded away, Rosa turning to give me one last snarl over her skinny shoulder as she left.

The envelope held a sheet of paper, covered on both sides with Errol's tiny handwriting.

GROWING WATERMELONS

Use Russian watermelon seed. Start the seed off in peat pots on a shelf over a radiator 95 days before you expect to harvest them.

Build three south-facing watermelon beds. They need to be seven feet by seven with wood walls three feet tall and a further two foot of windbreak above that. Set an opening in one of the walls and make sure you can fold back your windbreak to get into the bed. Make the windbreak of old sheets or fleece, anything that's white – whitewash the inside walls of the beds too.

Take out the soil to a depth of two feet and replace it with a mixture of equal thirds: well-rotted manure, home-made compost, good topsoil. Mound it up so there is a hill in the middle of each bed.

When the last frost date has passed, and each seedling has four leaves, put two pots in the ground on each hill. After two weeks, thin out the weaker seedlings and lay straw in the bed, so that it sits level with the hill. Don't compress it. This reflects sun back to the fruit and holds warmth.

Water daily – make sure the water is blood temperature. The best feed for watermelons is weekly liquid nitrogen until they set flowers and then a weekly potassium feed as the fruit grows. Weed through the straw as necessary but don't disturb the melon vine.

As the fruits grow, lift them off the straw by propping them up on foam sponges. Move the sponges every day to stop the melon getting pressure marks.

Harvest when the stem starts to shrivel.

I was puzzled. Russian watermelon seed? Nothing else seemed exactly secret or surprising. I turned the paper over. On the back, in even smaller writing, it said:

Bert said that the secret of his watermelons was that every morning he walked up to the allotment and peed in one of the beds, making sure that it went all round the outside edge of the straw. It had to be the first pee of the morning and it had to be done to each bed every three days. He said that the heat and the stuff in his pee made the melons grow.

I remembered Errol's dry sense of humour. But Bert did grow very good melons... could I persuade OH to go to the plot every morning on his way to work...? As I pondered what OH would make of the suggestion, and whether I too would end up in a home (for confused horticulturalists?) if I suggested it, my feet headed automatically for Bert's plot. Russian watermelon seed...

The melon beds were gone. The shed was empty. It was as if both plots had been spring-cleaned. Not a single watermelon seed lurked on a shelf or in a crack between the floorboards, and I did check.

I scoured the site, asking if anybody had saved any seed from Bert's last watermelon harvest, but nobody had – we'd all given up trying to compete, and just settled for eating the slices of melon he gave away so generously without making to effort to grow them for ourselves. I went through seed catalogues – there was no 'Russian' watermelon seed. Errol was pulling my leg.

Two years later, I bumped into Errol, visiting Maisie's plot on a rare visit from Bridlington. Rosa had died, and he was now towing around a small, fat dog that he insisted was a Bridlington Terrier although I was certain there was no such thing. I grabbed my chance as I walked him back out to his taxi for the journey back to his guest house.

'What are Russian watermelon seeds?'

Errol smiled gently. 'When Bert and I first met, I was in the New Zealand merchant navy, you know? So this one time our ship met a Russian ship on the high seas and when that happens you sometimes swap food and stories for a few hours. The Soviet ship had delicious watermelon and when I asked where it came from, they told me Siberia. When I told Bert this story he thought I was joking.'

'And?'

'It took me five years. I wrote to everybody I knew, asking them to get me some Russian watermelon, but back then it was a spying offence to do that kind of thing, you were risking your life, you know? Finally a mate of mine who'd gone to be a driver at the New Zealand Embassy in Moscow sent me some seed in an envelope. Bert treated it like pure gold.'

It was the answer to the question that I'd asked myself years ago. Whether or not Errol was teasing me over Bert's 'miracle ingredient', I recognised the emotion in Errol's voice as he told the story and understood why he'd made sure that nobody else would ever succeed in producing Bert's watermelons, grown with love, from Soviet seed, on a windswept allotment in Sussex.

Spring Plans

Spring is when most of us get ambitious about many things in life: running a marathon, getting married, finishing our dissertations, qualifying as a pilot or starting a family. It's also the time when allotment-holders get ambitious too, deciding that they will go for a gold medal in the horticultural show this year; produce their own grapes to make an amusing sparkling white wine; or just get to grips, finally and conclusively, with crop rotation.

The classic rotation system requires you to divide your plot into three sections of equal size, after abstracting an area for perennials like rhubarb and asparagus, then rotate your crops through the three families:

- Brassicas

- Potatoes

- Legumes, onions and root crops

This system immediately gives me a headache. First, legumes, onions and roots are not a family! Even in mafia terms, they could hardly be considered cousins, let alone closely enough related to be part of the same *cosa nostra*. Second, how much space do you leave for perennials? Third, what about the intermediate crops like strawberries which last only four years at best, three if we have a bad summer or they are in poor soil – do they count as rotators or perennials?

Even now I struggle with crop rotation and have to consult a diagram in the back of my allotment notebook that reminds me what is classed as being part of the same family, for rotational purposes. I've also worked out some cheats that help me keep my plot in good order without developing a rotation headache.

I found it easiest to start by working out what didn't need to be rotated. Many short-lived crops don't have to be counted in the rotational system, so you can plant summer beans (runners, French, wax and borlotti), annual salads, sweetcorn and cucurbits (courgettes, pumpkins, cucumbers, etc. – assume anything that scrambles along the ground and produces a balloon-like crop is a cucurbit), wherever you fancy. It's best not to plant them in the same place two years running but the world won't end if you do.

Then I put my perennials and short-lived perennials in demarcated beds. Some of these are purpose-built beauties like the many and various asparagus beds I've built on allotments over the years, while others are just a few bits of wood or some stones laid around a strawberry bed to separate it off from the rest of the allotment. This allows me to stand in the middle of the plot, in winter, and see which bits of the soil are not available for rotation. It stops me forgetting how far the strawberries actually extend and reminds me there are Jerusalem artichokes filling one area, even though they can't be seen through the mud or fog or driving rain.

So what's in each close-knit rotating clan?

Brassicas are Brussels sprouts, cabbage, cauliflower, kale, kohlrabi and things like pak choi and other oriental greens. In this family you need to include the humble radish (and the winter radish) and two of the winter roots: swedes and turnips. Why? I have no idea, but that's the rule – they may have a different-shaped nose and fail to have inherited perfect pitch like everybody else in the clan, but family they are, as far as rotation is concerned.

Legumes – peas and broad beans are in this 'family' as are all the annual onions, garlic, shallots and leeks and a motley collection of roots such as beetroot, carrots, celeriac and its taller cousin celery, fennel and parsnip – you can bung any root crop that doesn't feature in the brassica family, and isn't a potato, into the legume rotation and feel confident you've got it right.

Potatoes – this is a funny old family because it includes all the solanaceae (which is a mafia sounding name if ever I heard one) such as potatoes and tomatoes and for simplicity (trust me, it starts to make sense soon) I add the two other solanaceae cousins: peppers and aubergines. You can actually grow those last two outside the rotation system, but I find it easier to include them in with the spuds. Oddly, and for reasons nobody has ever managed to explain to me, the goji berry is classed as solanaceae, but it doesn't matter because if you're growing goji, you count it as a perennial, not a rotated crop. If it's all as clear as mud, don't worry, this is how and why it matters.

Assuming you've got the kith and kin relationships established, it's time to work out how to rotate.

First Year

Section one: Potatoes
Section two: Legumes, onions and roots
Section three: Brassicas

Second Year

Section one: Legumes, onions and roots
Section two: Brassicas
Section three: Potatoes

Third Year

Section one: Brassicas
Section two: Potatoes
Section three: Legumes, onions and roots

Why bother? The reasons for keeping the three families happy are crucial to crop success. Get rotation wrong and while for a time you might not see any problems, sooner or later, like a protection racket being denied its cut, the unrotated allotment will develop strange and devastating problems and failures. The rotation system, if ignored, has three ways to get your attention and remind you that you only grow with the blessing of the families. Invasion, starvation and collapse are the ills that will be visited on you if you break the rules.

Invasion: large quantities of the same crop, or large plantings of related crops, are a target for pests. A cabbage white butterfly certainly likes *a* cabbage, but given access to a complete row of cabbages it will go into an egg-laying frenzy, creating enough offspring to destroy the entire crop. Not only that, but like a lowly *mafioso*, it will tell all its friends that this place is ripe for doing over and bring them along to contribute to the destruction. You might think this isn't such an issue if you're non-organic because you can spray against pests, but even non-organic growers can't do much against the heavy-duty wreckers like disease and blight. If you grow your spuds in the same soil several years running, you end up with a plague of eelworms and slugs below ground and rampaging attacks of blight above ground. Rotation is the protection money you pay to avoid these, and other, invasions. Most pests are short-lived, so if you deprive them of their preferred food for a couple of years, their numbers will drop rapidly. By the time you do replant their host crop, there aren't enough of them to do much harm, and they don't get to proliferate because you then cut off their food supply again by planting something they can't subsist on for a couple more years. This is why turnips are in with the brassica family: they suffer from the same diseases, such as club root.

Starvation: just as the mafia cuts the supply lines of any business that refuses to pay protection, planting the same crops in the same place too often will destroy the nutrients in the soil. This impoverishment of the soil leads to the use of artificial fertilisers on non-organic plots or costly investments in manure and compost on organic ones. Regular alterations in crop families will ensure that plants using certain nutrients are followed by those that don't use or even replace those soil components. Some crops are hungry crops, like spuds, and they should be planted in newly-manured soil. Other crops are nowhere near as demanding, such as the legumes, and if they follow on from the spuds, they can actually add fertility back to the soil in the form of nitrogen.

Collapse: just as people living under a brutal regime tend to be dejected and depressed, soil that suffers the same processes year after year will tend to compact and lose its friable nature. This means that rain runs off it without penetrating the top layer. When the earth becomes impermeable it loses most of the potential value delivered by falling leaves or other plant material that decays on the surface. Where soil is completely compacted, worms and other soil-dwelling creatures can't even break through the crust to help oxygenate and soften the earth. As an example, most people firm the soil around Brussels sprouts to stop them rocking in the wind and therefore breaking their roots, which can lead to the sprouts 'blowing' and becoming open instead of tightly budded. The following year it's good to plant something, such as potatoes, that will open that soil, breaking it up and allowing nutrients and water to filter down into the lower layers again.

So, pay your dues to the mafia plant families and you'll be OK!

You can choose to ignore the rotation system, but only if you choose a completely different kind of growing, where you plant everything in together, all higgledy-piggledy and in apparent chaos. This is the type of planting that is sometimes characterised as cottage gardening, or, when it's more disciplined, as square-foot gardening. In every case, there's still a rotation system at work, but it's a more intuitive one – it relies on you replacing each edible you remove with an edible from a different family, thus rotating not by bed or area, but plant by plant.

Celia, my clever friend, was the first person I ever met who maintained an edible garden on permaculture, no-dig, principles. Since then I've come across quite a few people who try this system, but only one other who's actually managed to keep it going.

No-dig, permaculture, square-foot gardening, forest gardening and other planting regimes that mix all the plants together and rely on a complex ecosystem to keep everything going may be fork- and spade-free, but they are not labour-free. While they don't have the same inputs in terms of manual labour, they still have inputs, one of which is an intelligent and informed understanding of how ecosystems work.

Another necessary input is intuition, which Celia has in abundance, but many people don't. Intuition, in gardening terms, is partly an outgrowth of long experience, but mainly it's a mysterious sixth sense that some people possess and others never will. Sadly, the never-wills are also the ones most likely to opt for permaculture, forest gardening or some other form of vegetable growing that they fondly believe is good for the planet and won't require them to do anything they consider boring such as digging or heavy weeding.

Permaculture is a fantastic way of growing things, but it usually requires an advanced level of expertise in the grower. Like forest gardening, permaculture is based on an understanding of soil, climate and plants and their interactions, which is either obtained theoretically – through long study – or practically – through knowing your patch phenomenally well.

In Celia's case it's both. She dug and weeded her allotment for five years before turning it over to permaculture principles, and she's studied sustainable food production to a level that means she gets called by 'experts' who write for the Sunday newspapers to advise them on her particular specialism: seed dormancy and how to break it. In other words, she falls perfectly into a particular category of British eccentric – the gifted amateur.

To be allowed to sit Celia's plot I had to pass an informal viva, which she handled so delicately that I didn't even know I was being cross-examined. It wasn't my expertise she was interested in, so much as my ability to admit ignorance, and I passed with flying colours! A permaculture plot can be quite fragile, so Celia wanted a plot-sitter who wouldn't have an aberration and run wild with a pesticide, or dig up all her companion plants in the mistaken belief they were weeds. I was so busy soaking up the scents, sights and sounds of her plot that I happily failed to show what little knowledge I had, and therefore earned myself the label of 'willing village idiot', which is rather what I feel I've been, in Celia's eyes, ever since.

She sent me home from that first visit with a black basil plant and the memory of a pair of jays giving me the evil eye from the top of her quince tree. Celia had told me that the jays planted acorns and I was empowered to pull out any seedling oaks I found on the plot – I took this as a bit of leg-pulling but in the years I've spent plot-sitting for Celia I must have removed more than a hundred baby oaks and they are only the ones that the jays didn't remember to go back and eat!

If You Like Succulence...

Succulent crops such as early peas and asparagus are amongst the most popular to grow. Succulence is a food quality that most people respond to, and many wannabe allotment-holders yearn to grow their own crops just because they remember harvesting home-grown peas or strawberries when they were kids.

Asparagus is a delight to eat, but a little demanding to grow. Like a temperamental concert pianist, asparagus must have its conditions met, or it will refuse to appear. It will take at least three years from bed-making to cropping, so unless you're a natural nurturer, an asparagus bed can seem like a pit into which you chuck time, money and effort. If you think you can make the investment, though, it's a dinner party delight to harvest your own asparagus in mighty bundles to awe your guests – or just to steam a few stems to eat with a poached egg in front of a good film on TV.

Asparagus likes a sheltered, sunny site and most people make a permanent bed so that they can give this fussy crop the rich, well-drained soil it prefers – think of this as the grand piano from which the concert pianist produces glory. Raised beds need to offer a ninety-centimetre square of growing space for each crown, and you need a minimum of six crowns to give value to your investment. The topsoil needs to be either settled on a bed of grit, as the Victorians did, or to be well dug to at least thirty centimetres' depth with lots of coarse sand added before topping off with vintage manure.

Don't be tempted to beg/buy asparagus plants from other allotment-holders or grow them from seed. You want your crowns to be all male and while there are a bewildering range of varieties in the catalogues, nearly all will do massively better than the random offerings of others. This is because female plants, once established, will produce berries and then seed from around late August in their third year. That's a waste of energy which the male plants put into producing a vigorous fern that then feeds the plant's roots more thoroughly to ensure a better crop the following spring.

My favourite variety is Lucullus, although all the modern varieties crop well. There are two reasons I prefer Lucullus to other varieties: the first is horticultural – a Canadian study found that this was the asparagus that was most adaptable to a wide range of conditions. Their test was of different soils and climates, but it seems to me that the average British year could easily provide more climate range than a fussy asparagus could tolerate, so in opting for Lucullus I hope I'm working with a generous asparagus that will rise to whatever the weather throws at it. The second reason is that I love the idea of an asparagus named after one of the most influential and luxurious gardens, and gardeners, of antiquity.

Asparagus Production the Sexton Way

Try to get one-year crowns – a lot of people assume that as you can't harvest until the third year, it's better to buy crowns that are three years old and start harvesting in the first summer after planting, but for really strong plants that produce well for up to twenty years, buy babies and raise them yourself. Those first winters in your asparagus bed – when the plants establish feeder roots and get used to their individual conditions – give them the tolerance for your weather and soil that will allow them to thrive, giving you bigger crops than the impatient folk who bought older crowns.

Planting time for your crowns, which will arrive looking like freeze-dried *Dr Who* aliens, is between late March to mid April. We plant ours on a zigzag to make the best use of space, but if you've dug and gritted a trench, you'll be planting in a row. In either case, the plants need to be at least thirty centimetres apart, and with ninety centimetres between rows or forty-five between zigzags. Mound up the earth by about ten centimetres, then scrape a bowl-shaped hole around five centimetres deep for each crown and settle it in place, spreading out its weird spider's-leg roots before covering again.

You'll need to earth up the shoots a couple of times in the first summer after planting, so that the crowns end up between twelve and twenty centimetres under earth but still raised above the original ground level. This ensures the roots drain easily. A raised bed makes this much easier, as you just sprinkle some topsoil mixed with good manure or vintage compost into the bed to increase the depth, which in turn produces longer, more succulent stalks.

For two years, all you can do is weed and feed your asparagus bed. The plants will thrive on a dose of blood, fish and bone in April and on hand-weeding through the summer. We bottle-water our asparagus so that weed seeds aren't a problem. When I plant our crowns, I sink a 1-litre soft drink bottle beside each one: neck down, cap removed and with the bottom cut off. In theory the crowns are thus watered at their roots, and the surface of the bed sees no water apart from rain and dew, so weeds stand little chance of germinating. This is only actually true if I stand over OH like a regimental sergeant major, bellowing insults if he so much as points the hose near the asparagus bed. Given a chance, he will water the surface of the entire allotment, including the bottle-watered beds, and a fine crop of opportunist annual weeds will spring up that I have to hand-weed out.

In year three, you are allowed to cut every second asparagus spear you see in May, but you should then stop cutting. In year four, you can cut as much as you like from mid April to mid June. You wouldn't want to cut after solstice date anyway, as the spears become as woody as asparagus-flavoured dowel rods.

Don't tie up or cut back the foliage, it's just a neurotic Victorian tidying-up habit which interferes with the growth of next year's crop. Instead, let the ferns grow until they become golden in autumn, then trim them down to a couple of centimetres above the ground, weed for the last time that year, and top up the bed with a layer of well-rotted manure to act as both food and winter mulch.

Asparagus is an investment that you need to be sure about: the location is important, the quality of the crowns is vital and you have to be confident in your commitment to caring for your bed over the long term. Get it right, though, and it's like having a small treasure chest of green succulence.

If it sounds as if I have massive experience of creating asparagus beds, that's because I have. I've built and planted five of them in twelve years – and only harvested from one. All the others were on plots where I was a co-worker and for some reason wasn't still working the plot when the asparagus came to harvest. Belatedly, and shamefully, I realise that OH's constant refrain of 'it's not our plot' may be justified…

ASPARAGUS AND PEA RISOTTO

The succulence of asparagus is its own reward, like virtue, but you will always get some spears that are as skinny as string and seem worthless for anything except soup. They aren't, though – I've discovered how to use those ultra-thin spears, called sprue, in a delicious spring risotto that marries the succulence of asparagus to that of peas fresh from the pod. This recipe serves two as a main course, or makes a brilliant starter for four, if you follow it with a robust main course, and is one that we share every year with Celia and Stefan, who race us to produce the first batch of sprue for this dish. Regardless of which couple gets the earliest harvest, it's always me who has to cook the risotto, as Celia can't be trusted with anything as precious as asparagus!

INGREDIENTS

- Olive oil
- 1 white onion, finely chopped
- 1 garlic clove, minced
- 200 grams risotto rice

• 2 shallots (if you still have some left from the previous year)

• 600 ml vegetable stock or 500 ml stock and 100 ml dry white wine, heated together and at a simmer in a separate saucepan

• A handful of skinny asparagus spears, chopped into fork lengths, and a handful of peas (two handfuls if you really love them)

• 75 grams grated Parmesan and a little more for garnish

• Fresh thyme and parsley

• Seasoning

METHOD

Choose a large heavy-bottomed pan to make your risotto and begin by coating the base of it with a couple of tablespoons of good olive oil. When the oil is gently heated, add the onion, garlic and shallots and fry, turning, until soft and transparent.

Now add the rice and thyme and cook for a couple of minutes, stirring with a wooden spoon to coat the grains in the oil. Continue to cook for three or four minutes so the rice becomes a little translucent.

Add a ladleful of the stock and stir it into the mixture, continuing to turn over the grains. Keep stirring until the liquid is absorbed and then add another ladle of stock. A risotto needs constant love and care, a bit like asparagus!

Keep adding and stirring for about twenty minutes, then tip in the asparagus and peas and give them a good stir to blend them into the sticky, onion-scented rice. Add more liquid and stir for about a further five minutes – that's all it takes to cook really fresh vegetables.

Stir in the Parmesan and then taste for seasoning. Don't forget how incredibly hot risotto can be so blow on your mouthful to cool it before you try it. Add a little salt if necessary and some pepper.

Serve, sprinkled with the rest of the Parmesan and some chopped or torn parsley for colour.

Succulent foods have a particular mouthfeel that's almost impossible to describe, but if you like asparagus, the texture of a home-made fruit curd will probably appeal to you.

Plums are amongst the most succulent fruits and offer themselves to an incredible range of treatments. Apart from eating dessert plums fresh or stoning and cooking as a pudding fruit, you can try bottling, wine-making, drying, pickling, jamming, or making a fruit leather. We've never been lucky enough to manage an allotment with a mature plum tree, but Maisie's father was an expert in both soft and top fruit and so she regularly gives us buckets of plums. We supplement her generosity by foraging in the Sussex woodlands for wild plums, which have an unparalleled flavour but are much smaller than their cultivated cousins. The best way to harvest a wild plum tree is to give it a good shake and then pick up the fallen fruit – if you stand right up against the trunk as you shake the tree, you don't get hit by the falling plums, but if you stand further away, you quite often end up with overripe plums bouncing off your head!

PLUM CURD

This is a delicious treat with one potential downside – it doesn't keep for more than a couple of weeks. This has never been a problem in our house!

Start by making plum pulp. Put around 400 grams of washed plums in a saucepan and cook them gently until they soften and the skins begin to shred. Then allow them to cool a little before using a wooden spoon to push them through a colander placed over a glass bowl so that the pulp is broken up and passes through but the pits (which, in wild plums, can be so small they are more like pips) are trapped. You can make a similar pulp with apricots, peeled apples or peaches, but soft fruit like raspberries, redcurrants and strawberries have to be sieved to take out pips and cores, while blackberry or blackcurrant curds both taste fine but tend to be an unattractive pale grey-mauve colour.

INGREDIENTS

- 300 grams plum pulp
- 125 grams caster sugar
- 125 grams unsalted butter
- 2 eggs
- 1 egg yolk

METHOD

Add the sugar and butter to the glass bowl with the pulp and place over a pan of simmering water – I prefer to put the bowl on a trivet to avoid any chance of the curd sticking to the bottom of the bowl, but this is a 'finick' as my Grandnan used to say, rather than a necessity. Stir frequently until the butter is melted and sugar dissolved. Now whisk the eggs and yolk together and beat into the mixture. Nigel Slater advocates whisking lemon curd for a lighter texture, and I do whisk my plum curd, but this is another 'finick' – you can beat or whisk as you please!

Continue to cook, whisking or beating away, until the mixture thickens – you can test this by dipping a clean metal spoon into it and watching how it coats the back. You want it to stick rather than running straight off. If you're in doubt, unsure of your preserving skills or easily distracted, this should take about ten minutes on a timer.

Remove from heat, and while it is cooling, give it the occasional whisk (or beat!) to encourage the heat to dissipate and to stop it setting too firmly. When it is completely cool, pour it into sterilised jars, cover and refrigerate. A home-made curd keeps for a couple of weeks in the fridge, but rarely lasts that long, once people know it is there!

These curds are not as strongly flavoured as the aggressive lemon curd sold in supermarkets, and have a higher fruit content so they might be considered to be a bit healthier. Their subtlety lends itself to imaginative ways of baking and creating desserts, and they are particularly good simply spooned over vanilla ice cream.

Favourite ways to eat curd in my house include:

- Using curd instead of jam to fill a sponge cake.

- Curd tarts: simply cut large circles of puff pastry and put them in the fridge to relax while you grease the underneath of a metal muffin tray. Lay the circles over the mounds made by the upturned cups, and bake until golden and puffy. When eased off the bases, they are perfect receptacles for filling. We like to put a halved dessert plum in the bottom, top it with plum curd, and sift icing sugar over the top. Adults may appreciate it if you match the fruit with its alcoholic offspring by filling an upturned plum with slivovitz before adding the curd, or apricot brandy for apricot curd, etc.

- Make parfait with meringues from the leftover egg white (the easiest way to make a meringue is to beat the egg white lightly, then blend in icing sugar until it becomes a stiff, glossy paste, mould into walnut-sized balls, space well on greaseproof paper and microwave on high for one and a half minutes until the meringue doubles in size). Crumble the meringues slightly and layer or swirl them with whipped cream and fruit curd in a clingfilm-lined loaf tin and freeze for an hour. This makes a well-chilled but not entirely frozen dessert that can be sliced thickly. It appeals equally to children and adults.

Fruit curds make an ideal filling for a dessert omelette, and if you have a fruit jelly to accompany the curd, a spoonful of each on the omelette before you fold it gives a blend of tangy/velvety tastes and textures that really lift a simple pudding into cordon bleu realms.

Spread fruit curd on crumpets for a delicious children's after-school treat, or to cheer yourself up before leaving for work on a grey and rainy morning.

Gluts and One-Up-Personship

If you haven't read E. M. Delafield's *Diary of a Provincial Lady*, go and add it to your reading list. It doesn't matter if you're not a lady, and it doesn't matter that the book has nothing to do with allotments and was written in the 1930s, it's still one of the most instructive books on allotment life.

Basically, you will be the poor diary-keeper who features in the book: no matter what she attempts, she is always outdone by her neighbour, Lady Boxe, or undone by her family. When it comes to gluts and/or prizes, you will always be beaten by somebody a few plots away, and your family, friends and co-workers (if you're lucky enough to have any of the three left, after you've run an allotment for a year or so) will always still undermine and sabotage your efforts, whether deliberately or inadvertently.

Take the courgette. It is impossible not to grow a courgette plant – I have even had them appear in years where I have not sown any seed, because birds or mice have carried the seeds to my plot. Courgettes will become courge without warning, changing from slim-hipped soft-skinned green cylinders to bulbous, armour-plated bulges overnight. It's as if your courgette has been kept young and lovely by a team of allotment beauticians, and they all go on strike at once, so that by morning your courgette has undergone a Dorian Gray transformation. Courge is what French people call all kinds of squashes, and courgette is just the diminutive term, so it's a bit like the way cute kittens become monstrous feral one-eyed tomcats (and always choose the middle of your asparagus bed to dig a big hole and do something disgusting), which has never stopped anybody adopting a kitten and won't stop allotment-holders, for generations to come, from planting seven courgette seedlings when one alone would provide them with more squashes than they could happily consume.

You simply cannot eat enough courgettes to stop them glutting, and you cannot get rid of your courgette glut even if you pick off the flowers and cook them in batter (which is a sort of chi-chi pre-emptive strike on the plant), or try to bribe people to take the courgettes away with them. I know: I have tried. One year I succeeded in making people take a bag of courgettes along with every punnet of strawberries I gave away, but I still ran out of strawberries long before the courgettes were gone. You can make courgette pickle, courgette cake, courgette rum (choose a courge for this, it's just about all they are good for) and ratatouille every day for six weeks, and you'll still have a glut, and your family will have either left home or started ordering in takeaways every night before you get home from the plot, in an attempt to stop you pretending that the suspicious green bits in your home-made lasagne are 'thick-leaved basil'. At this point, all your courgettes are good for is boasting about, and that's where your own insufferable Lady Boxe will appear.

One year I went wandering around our site, gently intimating that I had more courgettes than anybody else, until I arrived at the plot being somewhat haphazardly tended by a woman who had three children and sunflower-printed wellington boots. I'd observed her from time to time, bawling at her kids and pinning up her hair, which tended to get tangled around her pea-sticks while she was picking peas, and thought she was a perfect target for my courgette boast. The idea lasted until I'd got halfway down her allotment path, littered with toy cars and dismembered dolls, and discovered that her children were playing war games behind a fort constructed entirely from courgettes. OK, there were a few courge in the foundation layer, but it was still mainly courgettes. I was out-courgetted.

If you have a freezer, you will have filled it with your first glut crop. On my allotment this is broad beans, if I'm lucky, followed by peas. I do not begrudge my broad beans and peas their space – I do not believe that there is anything finer than eating 'fresh' broad beans in November, or enjoying home-grown petits pois with your Christmas dinner. But it does mean that as the year goes on, and different crops outgrow their space and outlive their welcome, your freezer will be packed to its limits, your jars already filled with jams and pickles, and you will struggle to find anything to do with your surplus produce.

You may, at this point, start to think about competitions. I would advise you not to, as I've seen as many relationships founder on the Fruit and Produce tables as I have over urban adultery, but it's almost impossible not to spot a particularly large, lush, gleaming courgette and think that it's a prizewinner. Or it may be your superb strawberries, or your gorgeous French beans... whatever it is that gluts for you, it always produces a couple of perfect specimens that cry out for a medal.

So you believe. Trust me, you're wrong. Perfection is not in the eye of the beholder. Perfection, in produce terms, is a complex algorithm based on variety, weight, colour, texture, size and presentation. Note that last. Presentation. This is the word that could defeat you.

Yes, people do polish their marrows. Yes, they irrigate their strawberries with water tinted with aniline dyes that are supposed to add depth to the redness of the fruit, even though it may also cause cancers – who cares, they don't grow strawberries to eat, they grow them to win prizes! I have met allotment-holders who plant leeks in asbestos tubes, and others who clean their onion roots with toothbrushes and gently buff the skins with silk scarves before plaiting them (the onions, not the scarves). And those are just the wheezes I've learned about. There must be many more, so desperate or well-guarded that they remain secret.

The point of revealing all this technical trickery is not to give you an inside edge to competition winning, but to point out that a well-rounded individual with a happy social life would almost certainly consider this behaviour insane. If you are even tempted to enter such a contest, start by taking a good long look at previous winners and decide how much of your personality you will have to pervert or excise to be like them, because that's the path you are heading down when you enter a Vegetable Growing Contest. Of course if you win any competition this paragraph should be disregarded, because quite clearly all contests, in that case, are magnificent tests of horticultural skill and personal dedication, entered by heroes and won by superheroes!

I have never won even a certificate of merit in any such contest, but I have been on the judging panels of many, and the friction generated by the ill temper of the grower is transferred directly to the judges by some arcane process that makes the awarding of First, Second, Third and certificates of merit into a cross between a witch's inquisition and a court martial. It can take hours to decide if a score of 8.9 for weight ranks higher than an 8.9 for texture when two specimens are found to have equal marks. Measuring the girth of onions can be undertaken four or five times in a row, with different measuring tapes each time, if the judges cannot agree on the fractions of an inch that separate two contestants.

This all happens because judges know that they will spend the rest of the year being ostracised by the losers and patronised by the winners, which is why all allotment committees are so desperate to find visiting judges, as strangers won't have to endure the constant insults or smug complacency inflicted on a judge who judges on their home site.

I've never been a 'named' judge, although I've often been a panel judge: one of those lowly souls who weighs marrows and measures the circumference of leeks. I lack three essential qualifications as a 'named' judge – gravitas, status as a former prizewinner, and the tenacity to argue about the relative merits of virtually identical crops for hours on end – but I have spent weeks of my life ringing round allotment associations, horticultural societies, cooperatives, greengrocers, seed companies and even local council parks departments, trying to persuade people to come and judge allotment produce competitions. You can normally inveigle or shame local councillors, the Mayor, or a vicar, to come along and be a judge, but that's copping out. What allotment people want is a 'real' judge, one with gravitas, status and tenacity, so that they can feel genuinely recognised for their talent as a vegetable grower if they win, and proper bitter hatred of blood-feud proportions if they don't.

Back on the plot, even if the judge has been found and your beloved fruit or vegetable is peaking at just the right time, you can be certain your nearest and dearest will turn up and savage your carefully-nurtured prize specimens. It doesn't matter how often you say that you're saving a particular plant for exhibition purposes, your spouse or co-worker will always leave it until the last possible minute and then step backwards onto your best courgette, tip liquid manure over your onion crop or carelessly munch their way through your perfect soft fruit. And that will lead to recrimination at best, outright hostility at worst and has ended in allotments divided down the middle (and families too).

 ## Managing a Glut

There is a more decent way to deal with the whole issue of gluts. Actually there are two ways, and for the disorganised and faint-hearted I recommend the purchase of a black compost bin, into which you can tip your roughly chopped glut vegetables under cover of darkness. It seems like a waste and feels like a crime, but it is better than having to navigate past carrier bags of runner beans and boxes of wilting salad every time you enter the kitchen.

It takes a brave allotment-holder to destroy vegetables in daylight, which is why I would also recommend the purchase of a wind-up torch, so you can creep back to your plot at night and do the dirty recycling of veggies without your neighbours watching in pity or outrage. Unless, of course, they turn out to be doing the same...

The better way is to find out where your glut may be welcome. Possible recipients of your largesse include:

- Local hospices

- Food partnerships

- The Salvation Army (who particularly value salad vegetables that can be put into sandwiches in summer, and soup vegetables in winter, as that's what they serve to rough sleepers)

- Local schools (my county is rich in independent schools and while I was initially embarrassed to be telephoning them on behalf of the allotment site, I found that around a third of them were happy to take surplus vegetables to feed boarding students, especially if it was from an organic allotment-holder)

- Students (I know of one allotment site that takes boxes of food to the local halls of residence and leaves them there)

It does require a bit of courage to ring around and find out who will take what, but if you have an allotment committee, they can normally be persuaded to do this for you, as I know from having been persuaded myself! Alternatively, a local food partnership can be contacted through your council, and they often have a list of places that might take food donations.

BOBBIE'S SUMMER MEDLEY

If you grew up watching British TV in the 1960s, 1970s or 1980s you probably had some kind of summer variety show inflicted on you. These shows featured comics who were no longer funny, singers who seemed to be losing their range and something called the summer medley: a tinny pot-pourri of the summer's most popular songs, to which mediocre dancers would perform frenetically, shaking everything but their rictus grins which implied they'd been given lockjaw at the dress rehearsal and were going to expire as soon as the final curtain came down.

That's not the kind of summer medley I'm talking about. I mean the medley that fills your memory when you've had a perfect summer holiday and you can't explain later whether it was the sun, the sea, the food, the serenity, the sunsets or the good company that made the experience so wonderful.

Bobbie is my mother, and this is her recipe – her ability to cook great meals from whatever she has in her garden has been one of the formative experiences of my growing and cooking life. She based it on a dish that she ate in Greece and adapted it to our cooler climate and different crops, but it still has something of the exotic about it, like a ratatouille that's travelled even further than its brethren.

This one-pot dish should be made in large quantities – you can freeze several portions to use in different ways.

INGREDIENTS

Onions

Garlic – mince at least two cloves, or four if your family loves garlic

Tomatoes – cut in half and remove any woody areas near the blossom end then chop roughly

Root vegetables – the last of the early potatoes, a few carrots, thinned parsnip seedlings, etc.

Summer vegetables – lots and lots of sliced courgettes, an aubergine if you have one (chopped), some summer beans, the first of the peppers, still green. Just roughly chop whatever you have a glut of!

METHOD

It couldn't be simpler. Fry the onions lightly with the garlic. When the onions have become translucent, add lots of cumin, marjoram, oregano, sage, basil, thyme, rosemary, dill, fennel and a bay leaf or two. If you have a well-stocked herb garden, nearly all of these should all be around(ish) at the time you have your courgette glut. You may need to use store-cupboard dill and fennel from the previous year as they may not have ripened – and I will confess that I buy my cumin as I've never managed to grow it successfully.

Throw in the other vegetables, stir well, and cook over a low heat for twenty minutes before adding a pinch of cinnamon and a tablespoon of honey. Don't be tempted to fry the cinnamon with the other herbs: if you do, it will have a much more aggressive flavour and may overpower the dish.

Leave to cook on a very low heat, stirring every half an hour, for anything from an hour and a half for a large saucepan, to four hours for a pasta pot-full. It should thicken and soften and become rich and redolent of summer. When it's ready the flavours will be unctuous and slightly warming, like an extremely mild curry, and it will taste wonderful either hot or cold.

If you have a slow cooker, you can use it to cook Summer Medley in about seven hours, if you set the heat to low and take the lid off for the last hour, so that it thickens. Otherwise the sauce will be too liquid and insipid, a bit like the TV summer medley!

We eat this spread on slices of rye bread or I bake it into a puff pastry shell to make a posh picnic tart. It's also very good as a thick sauce for a chunky pasta, and at barbecues it makes a delicious topping for baked potatoes. We also use it as part of a Sunday brunch of Summer Medley, poached eggs and crispy bacon – a family favourite.

If You Like Sweetness...

My grandfather grew two kinds of strawberries: the big red luscious variety and tiny white alpine ones. One of my earliest garden memories is being allowed to pick and eat as many tangy white alpines as I could find. Today I grow both kinds too, but the traditional red strawberry has a special place on my allotment – two special places in fact, as I grow a June variety and a later one that is at its best in July.

If you know people who are unconvinced about the value of growing your own food, fresh home-cropped strawberries are a more convincing argument than words. There is simply nothing quite as sexy as a sun-warmed strawberry that has the complex fragrance of high summer and bursts against the teeth with a liqueur-like richness that is incomparable. Shop strawberries are a different and vastly inferior fruit.

Strawberries are pretty easy to grow too, and if you have enough space for a patio planter, or a front or back garden that gets reasonable sunshine, you can harvest your own luxury fruits. On an allotment you can go mad and grow enough strawberries to feed a Wimbledon crowd – they are one crop that really isn't difficult to find a home for, no matter how massive the glut!

Growing Strawberries

I plant my strawberries in raised beds so that I can control three things: soil conditions, slug and snail access and bird attacks.

Soil is important: too rich, and the strawberries just run up into leafy crowns; too poor, and the fruit are malformed and overly pippy. A raised bed or planter allows you to find the right balance. I enrich my clay soil with leaf-mould that I make from fallen pear and walnut leaves. Because strawberry plants generally only produce well for three years, I'm always getting one bed ready as another is in full production. The way I do this is to dig a barrow of manure into a one and a half metre-square raised bed in one year, and another barrow, half-compost, half leaf-mould in the next. In the final year I add half a barrow of sand to give good drainage, and dig it in well before planting out the strawberries.

Strawbs, as most allotment-holders casually call the sweetest of crops, do well in a location that has full sun for most of the day. If you plant in a raised bed, you can also control the breeziness of the spot, and our strawberry plants are always six to eight centimetres below the wooden sides of the bed, to protect them from the harsh Sussex coast winds that are likely to crimp their leaves and distort their growth.

If you are buying plants, you'll get a better yield from plants supplied between April and August. The ones delivered between October and April are often cheaper but they tend not to crop well in the first year, and as they're only good for three years, it's a false economy to buy winter supplied plants if you can afford the summer ones.

When your strawberries begin to form, appearing as small, green-white fruits – already bearing their full complement of seeds so that they look as if they have the pip equivalent of a hairy back (and front and sides) – lay some straw under the plants, lifting up the green-white fruits so they rest above it. This serves three purposes: it keeps them away from the soil, where slugs, snails and woodlice will eat them; it stops them picking up damp from the soil and becoming mouldy; and it creates a suntrap as the pale straw reflects back all the available sunshine to ripen the strawberries swiftly and evenly.

At this point you will also want to net the fruits, which is where having a planter or raised bed is really valuable, as you can more easily get some bird netting and drape it over a bed than you can arrange canes to support the netting and then stones to weight it at the edges. It's unpleasant to find your lovely strawberries have been pecked to bits by birds, but even more unpleasant to find that a bird has managed to tangle itself in your netting and is either flapping around madly or, even worse, has expired of panic. For this reason we always attach some shiny things to our bird netting: tinfoil, old DVDs, tatty old Christmas decorations that aren't even fit for a charity shop and so on. Anything that flutters and shines is likely to deter birds from trying to find their way through, into or under the netting. The Waitrose Woman (so called because she once turned down the offer of a Sainsbury's carrier bag to take her crops home, insisting that 'she couldn't be seen with anything but Waitrose') uses gold milk bottle tops strung together to make a garland that twisted and turned and definitely disturbed the pigeons.

Managing Strawberries

Assuming your strawberry plants don't get a viral disease, which is also less likely when grown in raised beds, you can continue to grow new plants from the runners of your old ones. In the first two years, cut the runners off as they emerge to keep the strength in the main plant – it's a kind of reverse Samson scenario! In the third year allow the runners to produce little strawberry plant babies and pop them into a flowerpot full of potting compost, pinning down the runners with a pebble so they root. Leave the potted runners attached to the parent plant until spring, then cut them free and plant them in the new bed. You'll get a slightly reduced harvest from the old plants, and none from the new ones, but in their second year those babies will start to produce fruit. Now you can lift and compost their parents, using the old strawberry beds to grow something else for several years so that you kill off any lurking viruses in the soil.

I prefer not to grow through plastic or membrane because I like the soil to be able to breathe. If you are going to try to keep a plot in as much cultivation as possible, covering and compacting soil and starving it of light and nutrients can be counterproductive. It means that you have to spend a lot more time getting formerly covered ground into good condition before you can grow anything worthwhile in it.

Once our strawberries are established in a new bed, I usually give the old bed a year of planting with annual flowers like borage and marigolds so it has a full complement of insect life and the surface has been somewhat broken again by the shallow annual roots and then bring it back into crop rotation by planting parsnips, scorzonera or celeriac.

Or, if you like strawberries, why not replace your exhausted strawberry crowns with some carrots!

Home-grown carrots are nothing like the tasteless watery things served up in cafés, nor the huge woody stumps fed to horses. Summer-grown carrots are sweet and dense, full of a sunshiny nutty flavour and definitely crunchy. Winter carrots can be less enticing, but there are ways to get around their bleaker nature.

Summer carrots are sweeter because they have more sugar in them, and they have more sugar because they grow quicker than their winter relatives. Sugar is converted to energy by vegetables, just as it is by our bodies, so the faster you grow something, the sweeter it will tend to be. The exception here is the parsnip which undergoes a Frankenstein-like conversion, becoming sweeter when it has endured a frost, but leaving that perverse root aside, the quicker you grow and eat your carrots, the sweeter they will be. If carrot greens are wilted, the carrot itself will be less sweet, so watch out for that when buying from shops and markets.

The smaller the carrots the sweeter they will be too. This is why Rebus-the-allotment-dog, as his name suggests, was welcome, while our other cairn terrier, Falco, was never allowed to visit the allotment – he would dig up all the baby carrots, mooch along the rows eating all the peas and then finish his devastation by burrowing under netting to see if he could find any early fruit. Animals can always tell when crops are at their best, and Falco would ignore the big carrots in each row in favour of their smaller, sweeter neighbours.

SUNSHINE CARROTS

Winter carrots can be a little dour. They are slow to grow and have thicker, more fibrous cores. But they can still be delicious if you use them imaginatively. We grow a lot of carrots and I've found ways of ringing the changes on this simple vegetable. This easy recipe offers three different finishing touches depending on whom you are cooking for: kids love the orange-flavoured version, adults enjoy the mustard variant with roast meats or pies, while the horseradish one works particularly well with fatty fish.

INGREDIENTS

- A bundle of winter carrots
- 25 grams butter
- 1 tablespoon maple syrup
- 2 tablespoons orange juice, or 1 teaspoon wholegrain mustard, or 1 of mild horseradish sauce

METHOD

Peel the carrots. Summer ones only need scrubbing but for this recipe you want them to take up as much of the sauce as possible, so taking off their less permeable outer skin helps them absorb the sweet juices in which they are cooked. Cut into batons, put in a medium-sized pan and add enough boiling water to just cover. Put a lid on the pan and cook for five minutes until they are barely tender.

While the carrots are cooking, melt the butter in a small pan over a low heat with the maple syrup. When the butter is liquid, stir in your chosen final ingredient with a small wooden spoon and remove from heat.

Drain the carrots and tip them back into their pan, pouring the sauce over them and popping the lid back on. Shake gently and leave for a couple of minutes to allow the carrots to take up the sauce, before serving with some black pepper ground over the top to bring out the warm flavours of the sauce.

Summer Holidays

When we returned to the UK from France with a newborn baby, we moved to London and I began to pursue my allotment dream. I soon realised that I might never get an allotment of my own, given the length of the waiting lists in my area, so I had to find some way around the system. Not only did I lack real horticultural expertise, I was working full-time, sometimes six days a week, so my value as a co-worker was negligible – most people want co-workers who can get to the plot at least a couple of times a week, if not daily.

I tried to work out if I had any advantages that could impress a plot-holder with my suitability. I came up with three:

- I could cook anything

- I was willing to give up my holidays

- I spoke French

There were strong Francophone communities in Tooting and Streatham, and Ghanaians in particular were keen allotment-holders. While they were charming, and would talk for hours and send me home with yams and okra from their greenhouses and recipes for making fufu (the West African equivalent of mashed potato, using cassava or yams), none of them needed a co-worker.

I put up postcards in the 'posh' garden centres and South London plant nurseries, offering to cook allotment produce in return for co-worker status, but I was no match for the cunning mummies. I 'auditioned' for four different women, cooking dinner party quantities of vegetables for one, making industrial quantities of jam for another. A third got me to produce gallons of blackcurrant cordial along with a summer pudding to feed eight. I can't actually remember what the fourth mum asked of me, but I vaguely recall pureeing beans, so possibly it was baby food.

In each case, I received fulsome compliments in person, followed by abject apologies by phone a day or so later. Each mum would have 'loved' to have taken me as a co-worker but it turned out her husband had already struck a deal with somebody else; or her nanny had signed up for a horticultural evening class and needed the plot for her coursework; or her brother had just lost his flat and offered his services as a vegetable grower in return for cunning mum's spare bedroom... in retrospect I can see I was slow on the uptake, and there was probably a mum's coven that passed my telephone number around on the basis that you got a day's free cooking out of this simple-minded woman, before making some feeble excuse about why you couldn't give her permanent access to your allotment.

My willingness to go without holidays turned out to be my golden ticket. In the beginning it was West Indian allotment-holders who handed over their precious plots to my then less-than-expert care. Trinidadians and Jamaicans living in South

London tended to visit the Caribbean for family events that seemed to last for at least three weeks, sometimes as long as six: far too long to leave an allotment untended in summer. Also, because they generally grew for an extended family, their plots tended to be in full production for most of the year, meaning that they needed somebody to harvest daily.

So when other people were taking their holidays on Ibiza or Ithaca I was packing allotment gear and tools for OH, baby boy and myself and catching the bus to Merton or Roehampton where we would spend the day weeding and watering, puttering and pruning and picking crops that we'd drop off with the allotment-holder's sister or cousin or aunt on the way home. Baby boy was cooed over by women who taught me how to make my own jerk seasoning and the arcane secrets of increasing the light and warmth available to grow tropical crops without spending money on greenhouse heaters and artificial lights.

Our 'holidays' became extended tours of allotment duty, and my name was passed around from allotment-holder to allotment-holder as somebody who could be trusted to manage a plot. From that first summer onwards, I was given plots to sit throughout the year. Winter skiing break in Davos? Kay will harvest your Brussels sprouts and plant your shallots. Easter cruise trip? Trust Kay to get your French beans started under cover. Taking a road trip across the USA in the long summer holidays? Kay will pick your courgettes, freeze your runner beans in conveniently blanched and sliced lengths and even sun-dry your plum tomatoes.

The trouble was that I had to fit all this extra activity into my life, along with husband, child and demanding career. It meant packing an extra bag with my allotment wear and taking it on my daily commute every day. After work, I would travel to the plot, change out of my Armani suit in the time-share shed and work for a couple of hours before OH turned up with a flask of tea and the baby in his buggy. We'd continue to cultivate until it was almost dark and then travel home together, our muscles aching, our fingers stained with bean picking and our toes dusty from the cracked earth, buckets of sweet-smelling tomatoes and bags of glassy peppers in the footwell of the car and bunches of short-stemmed late sweet peas tucked in around the baby's car seat like offerings to a junior harvest god. It was wonderful to spend hours in relative silence, weeding and watering, the baby sleeping in a shady corner of the plot or playing with nasturtium flowers or staring goggle-eyed at butterflies, and then to go home and eat a delicious salad that had been harvested only a few minutes earlier. It put the stress of London life into perspective and gave us some serenity in the midst of our demanding daily obligations.

Managing Your Summer Break

The simplest way to manage your plot through the most productive months in the year is not to take a holiday in the summer! This is the route taken by hardened allotment-holders and the one I use myself. If you book a summer holiday, finding the perfect plot-sitter is the best alternative to being there yourself. Assuming you can't get somebody to manage your plot while you're away, planning your crops to fit in around your summer break can help make your holiday a relaxing one, and ensure that you don't come home to an allotment that looks like a jungle.

There are two kinds of crops that are ready to be harvested in summer: the ones that can be left for a while without harm, and the ones that either spoil if left, or set seed, meaning that the parent plant puts its energy into seed production rather than into growing the part of the plant we choose to eat. If you simply must take a summer break, you want the former kind of crop on your plot.

Love and Leave Summer Plants

 Borlotti beans are pretty and simple to cultivate. Unlike runners or French beans, the Borlottis don't have to be harvested as they grow. Their mottled pink and green pods can be picked early and steamed, but you can also leave them on the plant to ripen, and then the pods become brown and dry and are thrown away. The beans inside the pods mature to become plump and solid. We leave our Borlotti plants for as long as possible in the ground, and then lift them, with the entire frame on which they've been growing, and put the whole thing on a clean old sheet beside our shed, away from the risk of rain. This allows the pods to continue to dry so that the seams start to crack, which makes it easier to extract the beans. In a good summer we don't have to do anything much about harvesting the beans, because by late September the whole bean vine is dry. When we shake the frame, all the beans fall out of the pods and merely need to be picked up and given a couple of days in a warm dry place just to ensure they are fully dry. The beans, when ripe, are cream with pink and burgundy freckles. Once dried, they should be kept in screw-top jars and rehydrated overnight before cooking. Because you don't have to pick daily to prevent them becoming stringy and dry, Borlottis are an ideal bean for those who want a summer holiday.

Welsh onions are also called everlasting onions – this can be confusing as there are two kinds of Welsh onion and only one is everlasting; the other is an annual. The way to tell the difference is that the flowering ones are neither true Welsh onions nor everlasting. The non-flowering ones propagate by division rather than producing flowers and seed. You can cut them like a chive, or use them like a spring onion by pulling up the small bulbs and chopping the green as well as the white part of the plant. As long as you leave some bulbs in the ground they will keep growing and dividing. Because they are much hardier than spring or salad onions they go right through the winter and will live indefinitely. This means you don't have to harvest them before the damp autumn weather causes them to rot in the ground, making them an ideal plant-and-pretty-well-ignore crop for summer holidaymakers.

Potatoes can be tricky as they need to be harvested in summer, but the unpredictable parsnip, once established, sits happily in the ground for ten months and copes without watering through a hot summer. The unpredictability is in germination: you can either grow parsnips or you can't. I can, which allows me to smugly recommend them to everybody as the root of choice. My parsnip germination rates are higher than almost anybody else's, regardless of soil or temperature, and that gives me my own specialism: I'm the parsnip lady! You sow your parsnip seed in February if your soil is light, March if it's heavy, and harvest from November or the first frost. You only have to weed a couple of times to stop the small seedlings being swamped and most modern parsnip varieties are problem-free, except for fanging (which just means they form multiple twisty roots) on overly rich soil or where there are stones.

Pot-herbs – these charmingly named plants were cultivated in ancient times to add flavour and nutrients to a salad (but not as a major ingredient, because they tend to be either bitter or a rather tough) or as an ingredient in summer soups. You can choose from Good King Henry (also known as Poor Man's Asparagus and very good when cooked like spinach), lemon balm (great for tea), lovage (interesting flavour which you either love or hate, said to be brilliant for the digestion) and sorrel (an astringent which can be invasive, so plant it in a bucket sunk into the ground). Because these are all perennials, you simply plant them, harvesting a few leaves in the first year and more in each subsequent year as the plant grows, but never so many that you risk killing the plant. They are low maintenance, high flavour, generally decorative and make a boring salad interesting.

Autumn raspberries are a good alternative to summer ones because (a) in my experience, they crop even more highly than their earlier relatives and (b) you'll be home to harvest them after your holiday. It's important to be fussy about varieties, because there seems to be a wider flavour range in the autumn fruiting varieties which may also perform differently in various parts of the country. I am a fan of Joan J, which I think has the best flavour of all the autumn raspberries, but it can fruit very early in a hot summer – as early as the second week of August, which makes it a bit of a gamble. Autumn Treasure has slightly less flavour, in my view, but can be trusted to produce most of its fruit in late August through to mid September which is ideal for those who like an August holiday. Autumn Treasure is also a robust variety – good news if you're an organic gardener, as it's one less thing to worry about.

LOVAGE AND LENTILS

This recipe uses two of the summer crops – lovage and Welsh onions – that tolerate summer neglect. It's also a perfect recipe to cook in changeable autumn weather, as these lentils are delicious hot on a cold day when poured on a slice of wholemeal toast and topped with a poached egg. Alternatively, if the evening turns sultry, leave the lentils to cool and serve them on some crisp lettuce with a topping of flaked smoked mackerel for a tasty cold supper.

INGREDIENTS

- 2 Welsh onions with their green tops, roughly chopped
- 15 grams unsalted butter and half a tablespoon of olive oil
- 350 grams Puy lentils
- A small handful of chopped lovage tops

- 1 sprig of fresh thyme, with the leaves torn from the twig
- The zest of half an orange
- Hot water with a splash of white wine

METHOD

In a fairly deep saucepan, gently fry the Welsh onions in the butter and oil. The idea is to soften them without letting them colour or become bitter. Add the lentils and stir into the onions, cooking for about five minutes, turning the lentils over so they become coated in the melted butter.

Add the herbs and zest, stirring to distribute, before pouring in enough water to cover the lentils. Simmer for around fifteen minutes, checking a couple of times to ensure the lentils aren't becoming dry as they take up the water. Puy lentils usually take around twenty minutes to become tender, depending on how old they are, so five minutes before the end of cooking time, give them a light sprinkling of salt, or a dash of soy sauce if you prefer, to add seasoning. Don't add salt at the beginning or the lentils will remain tough and hard-skinned.

Drain the remaining cooking liquid and reduce it to make a sauce, adding a little more butter, some black pepper and more salt if tasting the sauce suggests it's necessary.

How Many Beans Make Five?

S ome months after the water butt debacle, when the whole site was one big squelch, dotted with enormous and deliriously happy slugs making up for the dryness of early summer by wallowing in the rains of late summer, both the water butt and HSM's children came back to haunt me.

I was watching the rain turn the brick path on 'not' our plot into a small but energetic stream while I made broad bean pots. We plant our broad beans *(Aquadulce Claudia)* in the autumn to overwinter, as this saves them from blackfly attacks in spring. But because mice are always keen to turn wintering bean seedlings into gourmet dinners, we'd learned to give them a degree of protection provided by newspaper, masking tape and a libation of diluted Jeyes Fluid (or, if you're organic or don't like the smell of Jeyes, you can try ten drops of patchouli oil per 20 ml of water). Paraffin soaking used to be recommended, but to be honest I've never fancied eating beans grown from a plant that has been dipped in paraffin. If you've had peas or beans eaten by rodents, give the following method a try.

Using your favourite newspaper, make strips around forty centimetres long and twenty-four centimetres deep (sizes are approximate). Fold each strip in two so that it is around twelve centimetres deep and roll it around a small straight-sided glass container (I favour a Worcestershire sauce bottle, OH likes to use a tall tumbler) so that around two-thirds of the paper is wrapped around the glass and the other third extends past its base – fold this third up to make a neat bottom. Put the container down and press it firmly onto a hard surface so that the paper base is compressed and then lift it and lay a strip of masking tape across the bottom and up the side where the paper's edge is loose. Slide it off the container and you have one perfect little pot. Turn it so the base faces up and place it on a tarpaulin or old sheet. When you have made as many pots as you have beans (for peas you plant two to a pot, so you only need half as many pots as peas) and just before you sow your seed, dilute your Jeyes Fluid twice as much as the label suggests or use your patchouli blend and, with an old paintbrush, just put a small dab on the bottom of each pot – the aim is to give each pot the distinctive smell, not to soak the paper.

When the pots are dry, fill with your chosen seed compost, plant the beans or peas and water via the top, using a watering can with a rose attachment, rather than standing the pots in water to soak it up. The aroma, either of old kennel yards (Jeyes) or old hippy (patchouli), seems to be enough to deter the mice until the sowed plant germinates, at which time it loses its appeal for rodents and you begin to worry about birds instead.

We use the same system, but with a taller piece of paper and a wider 'base' such as a wine bottle, and minus the Jeyes or patchouli, to start our sweetcorn. Because corn is a notoriously fussy germinator in the amateur garden, we start it off in an unheated greenhouse, moving the small plants to a vented cold frame for several weeks before hardening off them completely and planting out.

As well as having diva-style 'needs' around germination – it does not germinate below 10°C (50°F) and the Super Sweet varieties insist on being a little warmer still; compost must be moist, but definitely not wet which can reduce the oxygen required for the seeds to grow; compost which is too dry will also prevent germination, so you're looking for a well-draining, slightly acid, damp but not sodden, planting medium – corn hates root disturbance. Getting our corn seed established in big, biodegradable pots that can then be planted out with minimal disruption has become our secret weapon in the who-grows-the-best-corn-on-the-cob race.

Anyway, there was me, some dampish newspaper, and a spider-infested shed window offering a view of HSM and her three bedraggled offspring heading for home with collapsing cardboard boxes piled with muddy beetroot and immense, hard-bellied marrows. The sight depressed me so much I went down to Maisie's.

Maisie's shed was full of home comforts: a battery-powered radio, a gas ring to make tea, swirly pink Novamura wallpaper and a window blind with a chirpy bluebird printed on it. Mainly though, it was full of Maisie, an experience I often found overwhelming. While she made tea and handed me a basket of shallots to separate and clean ('Nothing for nothing in this world' was Maisie's motto) I told her about seeing HSM.

'Do you think there's an HSF?' I asked. 'I mean, rationally there has to have been one, but is he still around...' My words tailed off as I received the full force of an old-fashioned look from my hostess.

'You haven't met him, then,' she said.

I shook my head.

'Well, let's just say it'll be an experience for you.'

She refused to explain, despite my attempts to cajole or trick information out of her, and changed the subject to her pet peeve – Felix. This was another area in which she withheld some information: the cause of their feud was a dark secret, although its daily progress was the subject of much allotment gossip.

'I see he's profiting from the misfortune of others again,' she announced.

'Who is it this time?'

'That new couple – the Sick Lady and her husband.'

I sighed. The Sick Lady had bought my water butt in the happy weeks before she became pregnant. Her morning sickness, at first a joke, had become a burden to her and her partner as it extended well into her second trimester. For the past few weeks neither of them had been seen on the allotment – Chaz had strimmed their grass path but their summer crops were rotting in the ground.

'What's Felix done then?'

'Well…' Maisie settled in for a good moan. 'You'll be as annoyed as I am by this one. They've given up their plot – did you know? Apparently she's in hospital and he went off in a tandem.'

I gave this some thought. Maisie's tendency to use approximate words could often make a conversation take a surreal turn. 'Tantrum', I decided, and shook my head in reply. If people wrote to the council ending their tenancy, the committee only found out about it when the council remembered to tell us, much to the annoyance of others on the waiting list who saw neglected plots and thought we were failing to re-let them in a timely fashion. 'That's a shame.'

'Yes, apparently she's been taken into hospital. The sickness isn't getting better, must be awful for her.'

We sat for a moment in silence, contemplating the poor woman's situation, and then Maisie got back to her story. 'You know your water butt?'

I sighed. 'Yes.'

'He gave them a tenner for it, cut it in two and sold half each to Compact and Bijou as water gardens, for twenty pounds.' She paused for emphasis. 'Each!'

That upset me. In fact I burned with resentment. Compact and Bijou were two of our newest allotment-holders and they'd divided their plot in two, front to back, with a picket fence and winding paths decorated with many gnomes. It was a byword for kitsch and cocktails and their attempts at cultivation were largely limited to turning up with half a garden centre in the back of their car, which they would then arrange beautifully around the plot, but without actually digging, hoeing, tilling, weeding or doing anything more than posing for photos with a watering can. In fact, they seemed to be mainly using their allotment for parties.

In the steamy comfort of Maisie's shed I could almost hear the plinking of rain filling up the 'water gardens' that should have been my reserve water supply. I wanted to feel properly miserable and thwarted, which is difficult when you're in a cosy shed, having biscuits pressed on you, with Radio 2 warbling in the background, so I headed out for the Sick Lady's plot to see if they were selling off anything else.

When I got there, the plot was bare – even the shed was empty – every pot and plant, tool and vegetable, had been removed. It was impressive: new plot-holders would be able to start planning immediately. Usually when somebody vacated an allotment the committee had to explain to prospective new tenants that they would be responsible for piling up rubbish to be removed from their plot and for ringing the council contractor to ask them to send a lorry round. It wasn't the best introduction to allotment life, especially if the previous tenants had filled their plot with rubble, old carpet and other annoying accoutrements to vegetable growing.

Chaz came past with a wheelbarrow full of holly clippings to strew over his broad bean seedlings in the hope of deterring birds. I pointed to the bare plot.

'It wasn't me,' he said automatically.

'Don't be daft, I know it wasn't you. But as long as you go around saying things like that, you'll keep putting the idea in people's heads.'

He shrugged. Chaz had been a one-youth crime wave until he was sent to borstal where he 'got' horticulture like other inmates got religion or despair, or an increased desire to get out and do it all again but without getting caught. Now he was in his forties and wore cardigans and rimless glasses that made him look like my old philosophy professor, except I couldn't imagine the professor pushing a wheelbarrow. I felt Chaz shouldn't hark back to his past, as it seemed like a permanent penance hung around his neck like an albatross, but sometimes it was almost as if he wanted people to remember. OH said that for a certain kind of man it was worth the suspicion and notoriety to have the credibility of such a background, but I thought that the instant claim of innocence was just a habit he couldn't break. It was one of the many things on which OH and I had agreed to differ.

The bare plot looked sad and ugly and I was reminded how oddly some people behaved when they had to give up their allotments. Sick Lady and her husband had only been tenants for a few months but they seemed to have found it just as tough as those who'd had their plots for decades. 'Stripping' a plot was one response: on one allotment site an expelled tenant actually hired a small bulldozer, lifted the topsoil from his plot and drove it away. Other common behaviours included simply walking away, leaving a shed full of tools and kit, plants in the ground and sometimes half-drunk cans of beer or cups of tea on the table in an eerie re-enactment of the *Marie Celeste* mystery, or 'touting' – where tenants who'd been served a notice to quit would go around the site trying to sell their equipment and even the plants right out of the ground.

Touting was legal but embarrassing – lots of people would end up buying something just to get rid of the evicted tenant whose complaints often made them feel deeply uncomfortable. The worse kind of touting, though, was when an allotment-holder died and their relatives would come to the site to take away or flog off the belongings of the deceased. It was always painful to see the beloved tools or plants of an old friend being removed, but even worse when a long-cherished implement was thrown aside.

Letting go of a plot is a painful business and I've had a lot of experience at it. Although I've been working allotments for nearly twenty years, in three boroughs and two counties, it took nineteen of those twenty years for me to obtain a plot of my own. For the previous years I had been a co-worker or a plot manager or a tenant's helper: all of which were polite names for unpaid labour, with little or no security.

Being a co-worker does have many advantages, but the one most often described is, in my experience, the one that materialises least often. Many councils allow co-workers to take over a plot that the tenant vacates, but in my experience this doesn't happen as often as co-workers would like, either because they didn't sign co-worker forms when they first began to work the plot, or because their local council lost the forms!

Alternatively, the very reason that an allotment-holder has taken on a co-worker can sometimes stop the tenancy transfer. It's relatively common for an older allotment-holder with health issues to take on a co-worker at the beginning of their difficulties and also to require the assistance of a family member on the domestic front. When the time comes to give up working their plot, the son or daughter who's helping out at home may very well offer to take over the plot too, which maintains continuity through the family, but cuts the poor old co-worker right out!

Another reason that co-working can be complicated is that relationships themselves are complicated. My best co-working experience was with an absentee tenant. The woman in question had recently divorced and wanted to enjoy life, but she knew that in a few years' time she'd be settling back down to domestic life (possibly with a second husband – she was certainly looking for one hard enough!) and she'd want to have her allotment in perfect condition when she was ready to take it on again. Essentially, while she lived it up and travelled the globe, she left me to run her plot. When she was home, I would drop off veg boxes at her front door, but she never interfered with my plans or visited the allotment. Her responsibility was to pay the allotment rent and mine was to run the plot. Giving that allotment back to its rightful tenant broke my heart – it was like handing a beloved pet over to a new owner, and even now, many years on, I have never been back to that allotment site, because I can't bear to walk past 'my' old plot. I am still friends with the allotment-holder though, and have always been grateful to her for giving me such a fantastic opportunity.

My worst experience was the 'Autocrat'. She was in her late seventies, small, wispy-haired and walked with a stick. I was amazed such a tiny lady could manage a plot at all, but her allotment was a fairytale space. It was garlanded with bindweed's giant white flowers and festooned with brambles that bore glossy black berries, which could wrap themselves around your ankle and rip your flesh to the bone. But if you looked hard enough, you could see that the seemingly forgotten space was sequinned with glorious islands of productivity: an autumn raspberry bed that offered sweet huge berries; a thicket of Jerusalem artichokes in which a horse could have disappeared from view; superb grafted fruit trees bearing velvety apricots or purple plums. The Autocrat said, in her terse way, that she could no longer cope with the plot and needed somebody to do the actual work under her supervision. I was enchanted by this Sleeping Beauty space and felt that the woman who'd created it would be wonderful to work with.

The enchantment wore off after a couple of weeks. Week one she required me to spend sorting out her shed, which looked as if she'd spent a century just opening the door and throwing things in. Week two was all about wheeling barrows of logs from the back of her plot to her son-in-law's car. He then drove the logs from the car park to her home, and her grandson split them and piled them in her garden for her wood-burning stove. In week three she asked me to take her shopping. By week four I pointed out that I hadn't actually done any allotment work, heavy or otherwise, and that I was giving up my Sunday, every week, to devote to growing things so, if she didn't mind, I'd like to start planting or at least weeding. She said, 'I don't know if you're suitable yet – young people are so impatient these days.' I started to feel like a Victorian skivvy being assessed by a stern housekeeper and fought not to bob my head whenever she spoke.

In week five she asked me to dig a potato bed. I did. She watched, leaning on her stick. I cleared and dug a space big enough to take seventy-two tubers in six rows. When I'd finished she gave me a lecture on my inadequacies as a digger and suggested I repeat the process on another area where she wanted to plant swedes. After a further afternoon spent digging, the Autocrat told me that my performance had deteriorated and she wasn't sure I was up to the job. Week six involved digging in manure for broad beans. I was, apparently, rubbish at it. She didn't say rubbish though; she said, 'When I said I wanted you to dig in shit, I didn't mean I wanted you to be a shitty digger.' It was witty, if a trifle cruel, and I tried to remember how to smile.

In week seven the Autocrat asked me to lay a concrete path for her. I asked why she would trust me to lay a path when she clearly didn't want me to plant, prune or harvest a single crop. 'Well,' she said, 'I don't trust anybody to touch my plants – I just want somebody to do the jobs I'm not interested in.'

I left the Autocrat's plot, never to return. Later I learned that she'd managed to inveigle at least four previous co-workers into 'working under her supervision'. One had built her greenhouse, another had long ago laid the path she wanted me to replace, a third had cut down and logged the trees I'd later moved from plot to car, and a fourth had dug the raspberry bed and built the frame that supported the plants. Not a single one of them had met her standards or planted a single seed. I think she was a witch. I also hope that when I am eighty and walking with a stick, I will be as resourceful as she is, although perhaps not quite so domineering!

Finally our allotment life changed and I was able to encourage OH to think of our current plot as really being ours, but the most I'd managed to achieve was to get him to say it was 'nearly' our plot rather than 'not' our plot, and only if I wasn't asking him to spend money that we couldn't recoup if it was taken away from us.

Our relationship to this new plot was somewhat more secure than that of a co-worker but nowhere near as guaranteed as that of an actual tenant because I was managing 'Nearly' our plot for the allotment committee. This meant election time was fraught, as a change of officers could mean the plot was taken away from us and given to whoever replaced me as secretary. I worried continually about this in the month before the AGM, although secretary of the horticultural association wasn't a post that people were fighting over. In fact, so unpopular was the post that I'd been asked if I wanted the job on an almost random basis: the plot-holder I was helping to build a shed passed my name onto the committee after turning down their request that she take on the job.

The next time I was up at her plot, I was confronted by a deputation that could have been chosen as the poster boys (OK, poster old geezers) for classic allotment anti-chic. The deputation consisted of three chaps, one in wellies, one in tattered trainers and one in hiking boots. One wearing the kind of hat that looks like a dead cat, another with cherubic ice-white curls, the third sporting a pony tail that looked as if it had been grown in the 1960s and never cut since. No trousers held up with string, but you felt that string-wearing was an option that hovered in the wings. As they made me an offer I couldn't refuse, I felt intimidated, then flattered, then worried. The intimidation and flattery soon faded, but the worry never really wore off.

I began by pointing out that I didn't have an allotment, and was years from the top of the waiting list. The committee told me that I would be secretary of the association, not the allotment site, so as long as I paid my membership fee, I could do the job.

I mentioned that my son had recently started at secondary school (hence my intimate acquaintance with the tuck shop) and might need me to spend time with him on his homework. The committee suggested I bring him up to the plot where he could definitely improve his biology and botany and he wouldn't be distracted by 'that internet stuff'. Their enthusiasm forced me to admit that from the day he'd turned ten, the boy had refused point blank to visit allotments, or even to eat vegetables that didn't come out of a supermarket-branded plastic bag.

I compounded my failure to pass the vegetable-growing gene on to my offspring by suggesting that a horticultural association secretary should have rather more substantial experience of this actual allotment site than a week trying to assemble a shed without the instructions (and, it turned out, three vital parts). The committee said that the association had members who didn't have allotments as well as those who did. I shrugged. They grinned at each other. I'd somehow been given the job.

It wasn't a difficult job, just an unpopular one. For several years, only part of the job had been done, the minuting the meetings bit. The horticultural association also ran the shop, inspected the plots, represented allotment-holders at meetings, and published a newsletter. The newsletter hadn't been in evidence for years, and taking it on was a daunting task, as I had no idea what people wanted to see in a newsletter, who the readership would be or how they would respond. Still, as I now spent my days putting words next to each other for money, I felt I should be able to cope.

Cope I did. When I'd been secretary for a year without disaster, the committee made me another offer – would I take on a plot that needed massive work to restore it to cultivation? They reckoned it would take about three years, and I'd only be a plot manager, but they would ensure I had a year of full productivity on the plot once I'd brought it back to life, and then they'd move me onto another plot that was beyond the scope of a beginner to repeat the process. The plot I left behind would be divided in two, and offered to people at the top of the waiting list.

I said yes.

Then I went home and cooked OH a steak and kidney pie and a treacle tart. He knew from the moment he opened the front door that I'd done something momentous, but he ate before he asked. OH has learned to experience my 'exciting news' on a full stomach: thus far, specially cooked feasts have presaged the news that we were moving to France, the information that we were expecting a baby and the announcement that I was about to give up my job to become a writer. The aroma of his favourite dishes now evokes a Pavlovian response in him – he sighs and frowns and makes sure he's had a second helping of everything before letting me tell him what I've done this time.

We'd been plot managers on another site too, many years earlier, when we were asked to take on a couple of plots on land that we weren't, for complex boundary reasons, qualified to become tenants on, so we knew what to expect. There are quite a few allotment sites that, for legal reasons like covenants or bequests, can only accept tenants from very small catchments. These sites find ways around their limitations by taking on plot managers or community co-workers to keep the land in cultivation. It's worked brilliantly for us, but usually it requires you to be a pretty experienced grower and to take on a plot that has problems. It's a bit like being a foster parent for a child with complex needs, but if you're dedicated, determined and willing to accept that you have no security, it's a route into allotment life that doesn't require you to have put your name down at birth, as with Eton, and it can be a superb way to get some of those intractable bits of an allotment site back into productivity.

Little Dibbers

The water butt fiasco caused me to spend several days lurking in my shed, fuming. But having made a *Guardian*'s worth of pots, I was able to enjoy the warm satisfaction that comes from having used to good purpose something that others would have thrown away – *had* thrown away, to be honest, as our pot-making supplies were generously donated by the local shopkeeper, who handed over damaged newspapers with a confused smile. Perhaps he thought we ate them. I'd sometimes wondered about explaining, but I was worried he might consider our bean pots too boring, or beneath the standing of a liberal newspaper. Funnily enough, conservative broadsheets never seemed to get torn. Perhaps they were tougher, or maybe he had clients for them too: men who approved of hunting and used damaged copies of the *Daily Telegraph* to make papier mâché duck decoys.

Anyway, I had a wobbly tower of pots: those at the bottom were several weeks old and already yellow and crisping from exposure to air, while the top ones were as soft and white as a field mushroom. The rain had finally stopped, after a week of incessant inundation, so I decided to do what I should have done days ago, and went off to Lola's plot.

Lola was an allotment baby. I'm pretty sure she wasn't actually conceived on-site (her pleasant parents, Rachel and

Steve, didn't seem the alfresco type) but Rachel had worked their plot until the day before Lola was born and was back four days later with the baby in a sling, taking it easy while Steve planted onions. Lola was three and a half now and we'd soon be losing her to nursery school, but until we did, she was our allotment mascot and portable sunshine. Seeing Lola always made me smile.

Her name wasn't really Lola, it was Emily, but around the age of two, for unknown reasons, Lola had started to dance. If you sang 'Copacabana' to her, she'd go into a bandy-legged stomp, her elbows level with her ears and her bottom lip stuck out in concentration. No other tune was guaranteed to elicit the dance but as soon as you got to the 'Copa... copa-cabaaaaaana', Lola would put on her moves. It was the most charming thing in the world to watch this little moppet tottering her way through a show-tune. Among my more surreal experiences was to look up every so often from my allotment labours to see the same gnarly, tank-top-wearing old codger who'd once hogged the water tank now bending down, with painful effort, to get into Lola's visual range before crooning out the sentimental lyrics, just to see our own little showgirl strut her stuff. It was a side of the old devil that I would never have suspected, not least that he knew all the words!

Nearly every allotment site has a Lola, and I wonder what happens to them – do they become self-conscious about their green playground once they're embedded in the materialistic world of school, or is it that their parents begin to worry that they are raising a feral child fit only for vegetable companionship and force them into the clutches of the Wii and other 'virtual' experiences? I don't know where they go, but I want to believe that the Tims, Sarahs, Peters or Beckys who end up quietly running the plots of the bossy women are actually little Lolas, all grown up and reintegrated with their allotment selves. In any case, Lola would be the perfect antidote to the lingering unease I was feeling about HSM's morose children.

When I got there, Lola was playing in the shed while Rachel stood outside, washing carrots in a bucket of water. Lola offered me a drink from her beaker, which I declined. She returned to her game which seemed to involve giving a lecture in a made-up language to some soft toys she'd stuck in flowerpots. I lurked, half in and half out of the shed, and chatted to Rachel.

'The Sick Lady and her husband have gone,' I said.

Rachel nodded. I tried (and failed) to suppress my inner satisfaction that some of her carrots were fanged.

'Maisie said that the husband went off in a tandem,' I offered.

Rachel thought about it.

'Tangent?' she said.

'I thought tantrum.'

'Maybe. She told Steve last week that the latest inspection really put a cat in the hornets' nest.'

We grinned at each other. Putting cats in hornets' nests was one of Maisie's favourite habits and collecting Maisieisms was one of ours. I'd missed the occasion when Maisie told a bemused plot-holder to buy twice as much compost as he thought he needed because 'you might as well be hung with a sheep as with a lamb' but we'd both been present during a famous site inspection when she informed the council allotment officer that every year she made her husband dig over the plot before she put her winter crops in, because it was 'good for his brassica disease'.

'Isn't that a bit risky?' asked the allotment officer, clearly worried he might be sued if hubby died of brassica-related complications.

'No,' said Maisie robustly. 'Anyway, if it's kill or cure, then whatever doesn't kill him is sauce for the gander.'

On that day, Lola was wobbling around on toddler reins (as per rule 10.1 *Dogs should be kept on short lead or otherwise restrained at all times* – Lola wasn't a dog but there wasn't a clear rule about children, so Rachel had sensibly applied the dog protocol to children) so it was left to me to trail casually after the inspection team until they were out of Maisie's earshot, when I was able to explain that we were pretty confident that Mr Maisie actually had vascular disease and Maisie wasn't trying to bump him off.

Rachel had now finished the carrots and began cleaning her hand tools, prior to going home. 'We got that rake from the Sick Lady's plot,' she said, pointing to the shiny new implement hanging on the shed wall. 'A tenner with a packet of compost activator thrown in.'

It was a bargain. If Sick Lady's husband had sold off all their tools and trimmings at similar prices then a lot of allotment-holders had saved themselves a tidy sum.

'Felix bought the water butt and the deck chairs,' she added, straight-faced. It was impossible to tell if she knew about the water butt's dark history but given how gossipy most allotment sites are, I had to assume that everybody, including OH, now knew how I'd been thwarted.

I nodded casually, as if none of this interested me. 'Good for him,' I said.

'He says he's going to offer the deck chairs back to the new plot-holders. It's being divided into two half-plots so he's sure one lot or the other will want chairs.'

Felix's entrepreneurial spirit was definitely getting on my nerves and I could understand why Maisie had a feud with him – he was bloody annoying at times. 'Do you think Maisie's problem is that she sold Felix something at cost that he then sold on at a profit?' I asked.

Rachel kept her expression neutral, which was nice of her, given how I'd just managed to allude to my own sordid water butt shenanigans.

'Maybe,' she said, 'but I don't think that would worry her. She's not in it for the money.'

The savings to be made by growing your own were much touted by local councils and some cheery garden writers, but our site had any number of plot-holders who were also freelance workers and kept careful cost analyses of their expenditure. So far, not one of them had tipped into the black, except one year when Felix (of course), who lived in a vast block of flats, sold enough bundles of fresh asparagus to other residents to turn a small profit on his plot's costs that year.

'Who is?' I asked rhetorically, but Rachel's answer surprised me.

'HSM,' she said.

I blinked. 'Really?'

'I saw her at the farmers' market. She's got a stall there, selling home-made bread and preserves – mainly chutney.'

Well, that explained why she'd grown such a surfeit of marrows: along with courgettes, marrow flesh is the easiest way to bulk out a preserve because its innocuous watery nature readily takes on any strong flavour and cooks down quickly to the right pulpy consistency.

'Isn't that illegal?' Rachel's question reminded me that I was an officer, an honorary crusty, and consequently expected to know everything about matters horticultural, a situation that gave me night terrors on a regular basis. This question was a rules one, not a growing one, so all I had to do was leaf through my mental inner rule-book.

'Nothing against it in the association rules,' I said, 'but disallowed by the council (rule 5.1 *Tenants must use their allotment for their own personal use and must not carry out any business or sell any produce from it, unless sold for the benefit of charity or the allotment association of that site*) as is just about everything Felix does! Still, Felix never gets caught…'

There was a long, uncomfortable silence in which Rachel fiddled with a dibber and I pretended intense interest in Lola's flowerpot toys.

'I could have been mistaken,' Rachel said slowly.

'She could have been minding the stall for a friend who'd popped to the loo,' I suggested.

'Or it could have been her sister. I mean… some people look very like their siblings.' Rachel was not a natural liar but she was doing her best with relatively unpromising material. I decided to help her out.

'It's a real pity you won't be going to the market again, because if you were, you could have found out for sure.'

'Oh but we probably will, it's very handy…' Rachel's words tailed off as she took the full force of my old-fashioned look. It was the same one Maisie had used on me and now I knew what she'd meant by it: the hole you find yourself in is plenty deep enough, so stop digging.

'On the other hand…' Rachel wasn't any better at improvising than she was at lying. 'It was very difficult to… to…'

'Park? Find what you wanted? Get home with your shopping?'

To each of my intelligent suggestions, Rachel offered a helpless shrug and headshake: she really was crap at dishonesty.

'Make the time? Manoeuvre the buggy around the stalls?'

More headshakes. Then she took a deep breath and went for it. 'It was very difficult to… um, choose between so many lovely stalls selling similar things.'

I stared at her, totally wrong-footed.

'So it would be better not to have to choose at all, by not going there again,' she continued.

As an excuse it was feebler than an unwatered seedling, but her commitment to honesty was impressive so I gave her a round of applause. Lola must have seen me because she joined in enthusiastically and was still clapping away with starfish hands as Rachel strapped her into the buggy for the journey home. Strictly speaking, Lola didn't need the buggy, but Rachel did, to carry all the vegetables she'd harvested. It wasn't unusual to see Lola hanging onto the side of the chair with a bag of spuds strapped into her place.

I waved goodbye and returned home, wondering what on earth HSM, with her anti-capitalist credentials, was doing profiting from her allotment and whether, as association secretary, I should say something to her about it. I decided the matter could wait until the next monthly market when I would have the chance to investigate for myself.

Where There's Muck...

Before the next farmers' market I found myself waiting for muck with Felix. The muck man would only deliver to a plot if the plot-holder was on hand to pay him cash for the delivery and was difficult to pin down to delivery days, let alone times, so it was necessary to lurk around the main gate with a pocketful of tenners, waiting for him to turn up. 'Nearly' our plot had eelworm-ridden, nutrient-depleted, close-to-barren soil and I'd ordered half a lorryload of horse manure to be dumped at one end of the plot so I could barrow it to the most infertile spots. Wheelbarrow work was my prerogative as OH's long spine had made clear it didn't do stooping, barrowing or heavy lifting from ground level.

'Are you the other half load?' Felix asked.

I waved my tenners in answer.

For a while we discussed crops, staying well away from the subject of watering, then we fell silent. After a few minutes of internal debate, I asked Felix what I'd always wanted to know. 'Why does Maisie hate you so much?'

He shrugged, but it was an 'I don't want to talk about it' shrug, rather than an 'I don't know' one, so I persisted.

'Did you two have a... thing?'

Felix snorted. 'Me and Maisie? What about Mr Maisie?'

'He only comes up here once a year and Maisie's very buxom,' I countered.

'No we didn't have a "thing"! I'm shocked you could even think it. What put that into your head?'

I stayed silent.

'Oh, I see. That's the gossip, is it? Some dirty-minded perv has decided Maisie and I were shed swingers?'

I filed the phrase *shed swingers* for future exploration and looked up and down the road for the muck lorry, as if I didn't want to commit myself to a comment.

'Oh come on! You can't believe that! Maisie's not my type!'

This time I raised my eyebrow at him. Felix huffed furiously and then, as I'd hoped, gave in.

'OK, I'll tell you what happened, but as far as I'm concerned it was all completely legit.'

I nodded, alerted to a dodgy deal in the offing. Felix only said 'completely legit' when something was distinctly off-colour.

'She said I took some cuttings from her plot without her permission.'

I waited.

'That's it.' He stared at me, defying me to disagree.

'No way! Nobody is that petty. What cuttings?'

He muttered something about it all being a misunderstanding.

'What misunderstanding?'

'There were some golden raspberries that had suckered over onto my plot and Maisie said I'd pegged them down to make them root, but I swear they just did it on their own.'

I called up my mental picture of their two plots. 'That can't be right. Maisie's raspberries aren't on the boundary you share; they're way over the other side of her plot.'

'They are now,' was his grim rejoinder, and he refused to say anything else until the muck man arrived.

Later, as I was spreading out the muck on 'Nearly' our plot, I tried to work out why Maisie might have been so unreasonable about a few cuttings, something that many allotment-holders were only too willing to share. Admittedly, Felix's ability to make money out of almost any situation was incredibly annoying, but Maisie wasn't usually mean-minded. It was a complete mystery.

I knew only one allotment-holder better equipped to ferret out a mystery than myself, so I took a break from my barrowing and walked over to Celia's plot.

When we'd moved from London to Sussex I began my allotment quest all over again. The boy was by now in primary school, OH had found a new job, and I learned to commute with the dawn, often coming home after dark. In summer, whenever I saw allotments from the train window I'd got off at the next stop to trudge back in my business heels to put a sign on the gate offering my services as an expert co-worker with good references. This was how I'd met Celia.

By now Celia's allotment should have been as familiar to me as my own, because of all the plot-sitting I'd done for her, but it wasn't. My relationship to her plot was one of confused awe and trepidation and each time she asked me to plot-sit I had to buy a new notebook to record the complexities of her current crops. Celia was a heritage seed saver, a remedy recorder and an amateur plant breeder and her allotment was a combination kitchen garden and apothecary's resource centre.

At any given time there were crops being grown in isolation cages, polythene tunnels that required me to wash my hands, cover my hair and remove my boots before entering, through to plants that had to be hit with sticks or shaken daily, and others with seeds that must be harvested then charred, or frozen or buried in a box of cat poo before being replanted to achieve germination. I was convinced the cat poo scenario was a joke at my expense until she showed me the eleven-page horticultural notes that accompanied the rare and precious seed, and I recognised the name of an expert in Amazonian botany whom I'd met professionally several years earlier. He'd been invited to speak at a conference I'd organised, examining the role of patents in the ownership of newly discovered plants. At the time I was running a think tank researching global problems and we'd decided to look at genetic diversity and plants. It's quite shocking to realise that plant hunters still exist, employed by major pharmaceutical companies to try to find 'cures' for major diseases by 'discovering' and taking ownership of previously unrecorded plants from the jungles, deserts and oceans of the world.

Conferences were one thing, plant conservators were something else entirely. I could cope with giving a PowerPoint presentation to 600 American business leaders or arguing with a customs official about admitting an ethno-botanist with a real shrunken head to the UK to give a lecture on the leather-curing powers of certain New Guinea plants, but being involved in the work that actually kept rare plants in existence gave me a sense of wonder and apprehension. This explained why, despite visiting Celia's plot a couple of times a month for several years, I'd completely failed to see a vast allotment site on the other side of the road. I swear my nervousness about inadvertently killing – or even worse, unintentionally cross-pollinating – one of her precious plants meant I always arrived at her plot in a state of mild panic that kept me blind to my wider surroundings. It wasn't until she took me to buy straw to lay under her pineberries (picture a white strawberry, with crimson seeds and tasting of pineapple) that I discovered the vast allotment site that was now my second home and hosted 'Nearly' our plot.

Being on the other site meant that I had to cross the road to get to Celia's plot, but that wasn't necessarily a bad thing, as it gave me time to stop and think. While Celia looked fragile, spoke gently and often appeared to drift around in an ethereal cloud of her own making, she was impatient of stupidity. Sometimes I'd get to the entrance to her allotment site and decide I'd rather go home and look up my query in a book than subject it to the ironic politeness with which she greeted my more asinine questions. On other occasions I would hear her cursing quietly but fluently in one of the many languages she spoke (Macedonian, Serbian, Croatian and Russian, in order of preference) and make a stealthy about-turn. A cursing Celia was a bad sign, and best avoided.

As well as translating complex legal documents into the four languages listed above and growing rare and endangered seed for fun, Celia completed the *Times* crossword most days. She was definitely an intellectual problem solver, which was why I hoped she'd help me pick through the two problems on hand: one, HSM and her market stall, and two, Maisie and Felix's feud.

I laid out the two cases in front of her, like Watson delineating a new mystery to Sherlock Holmes, and then got on with the task she'd set me – grading a bowl of not very interesting round seeds into three sizes: large, medium and small.

Celia worked silently for a while, counting seed into packets.

'Tell me what you know about HSM,' she said.

'Well, she's married, and when I asked Maisie about the absent HSF she gave me an old-fashioned look.'

'HSF?'

'Home-Schooling Father.' Celia nodded and I continued.

'HSM spends a lot of time on her plot with their three children: Portia, who's about nine, Reatta, who's about seven and Ayar who's probably four or five. She grows a lot of produce which I'd assumed was for self-sufficiency reasons but now seems to be for profit. That's illegal of course, and if she gets caught—'

Celia held up her hand and I stopped.

'Tell me about the children again,' she ordered.

'Portia, Reatta and Ayar. Home-schooled, always a little grey and wistful-looking but that could be because their mother makes their clothes. Kids in hand-dyed, hand-knitted stuff always look a little like refugees, don't they? Not allowed to eat cake, made to work quite hard on the allotment.'

Celia was nodding but I could see her mind was far away. A squirrel ran along the top of the brick wall that formed the rear boundary of her plot. She pulled a golf ball from her pocket and threw it at the rodent. The near miss sent the squirrel off at a run. The golf balls came from the playing field beyond the wall. For a long time the brick-built hut behind the wall had

been used by the school behind the allotments. Then it had lain empty. Recently the playing field had been brought into public use and the hut turned into a junior golf club, hence the golf balls and hence Celia having replaced all her glass cold frames with polycarbonate ones.

Now the stray balls got returned haphazardly to the driving range after serving as squirrel deterrents. The squirrels took it with good humour, sometimes seeming to hang around on the wall until Celia noticed them and lobbed a projectile. The whole process was a bit formulaic and half-hearted, as if both rodents and allotment-holders were taking part in an ancient rite that neither side believed in, and the squirrels were much more scared of the jays who mobbed acorn-thieves whenever possible.

I straightened my spine, which was suffering under the combined assault of wheelbarrow duty and seed sorting. Celia's neighbour, a silent old codger who grew magnificent spuds, prizewinning leeks and not much else, gave me a pitying look and I suppressed a groan. Damned if I was going to look feeble in front of an octogenarian!

Celia finished scraping seeds into envelopes and sealed each one with masking tape. Like many seed savers, she was obsessive about not letting moisture near her harvested seeds – even to the point of not using the lick and stick strip on the back of the packets.

'If you went to the farmers' market, would you have to report the HSM if you saw her running a stall?' she asked me.

'No, I don't report to the council, I'm only an association secretary, but if anybody asked me about it, I'd have to be honest about what I'd seen.'

'You can't go then.' My fragile-looking friend was suddenly steely. 'I'll go. We need to get to the bottom of this.'

'Well...' I was instantly fearful for HSM: not many people withstood a full-on Celia attack, a rare but devastating experience.

'The poor woman's obviously being mistreated,' Celia continued.

I gaped. 'How did you come to that conclusion? She doesn't seem mistreated to me. If anything, she's the one who's mistreating her poor children: they don't seem to have much fun, I can tell you.'

'We'll see,' she said. 'but I'm sure I'm right, from what you've told me.'

'And what about Maisie and Felix?' I asked, letting my sarcasm show. 'I suppose you've worked that out too.'

She closed her eyes and pushed her hands deep in her pockets, a typical Celia response. Sometimes, when somebody had asked her an unusually difficult plant-related question, I could almost hear the pages turning in the immense herbarium of her memory.

'How long ago did the feud start, do you think?' she asked.

I did a bit of cogitating of my own. 'They used to get on fine, according to Errol. You remember Errol?'

'Errol the chrysanthemums,' Celia said, eyes still closed.

'That's right, Errol the chrysanths. Anyway, before he moved away he told me Maisie and Felix used to be great friends, back when Felix had a girlfriend.'

'Lorna,' Celia supplied. 'She was called Lorna.'

'If you say so. Anyway, first Felix fell out with Maisie, then some time later he fell out with the girlfriend and she left. Don't know how long ago that was though.'

'I do,' said Celia. 'And yes, I think I've worked it out. See if you can find the records for the produce classes at the South of England Show in... ninety-five to ninety-eight.'

'Why?'

'Because the answer could be in them,' she replied and refused to say any more, so I returned to my barrow no wiser than before – if anything, considerably more confused.

If You Grow It, They Will Come...

I had a happy dream that we would become one of those families that foregathered around the kitchen table, shelling peas or stringing currants, describing our days to each other. It's possible that the rosy glow surrounding this picture came from having an overactive imagination, or perhaps from the oil lamps that my family, in my imagination, was using to illuminate their vegetable odyssey. Either way, it certainly wasn't a realistic view.

My fruit and vegetables are certainly popular, but mainly with the kind of creatures that Roald Dahl found attractive: bugs, creepers, scurriers and slimers. It was as if my plot had a large sign, invisible to me but glowing neon to every pest and repellent insect, saying 'free food and lodging here'.

There were invaders I'd expected: cabbage white butterflies, slugs and snails, carrot flies, ants, pigeons. There were invaders I'd hoped to avoid: wasps, mice, cats. There were even invaders I hadn't known I should have been expecting and hoping to avoid, such as eelworms, cutworms, wireworms – in fact any kind of worms: I was starting to fear that giant *Dune*-style worms complete with riders were likely to turn up. The final straw was a blight of *Lilioceris lilii*, the scarlet lily beetle, when I didn't even grow lilies! I began to feel like Donald Rumsfeld describing known and unknown and known-unknown perils to a dubious audience, not to mention the unknown-unknown where the damage to plants could be seen but the damage-causer was no longer in evidence to be identified, and maybe, combated.

As with everything in life, prevention is the best route. Not the simplest, not necessarily the cheapest, and almost never the first route taken, but just about always the best one. Crop rotation stops many pests getting a good grip on your plants, and while that's great news for the established allotment-holder, for the person taking over a plot, or the new allotment-holder whose growing area has just been carved out of former agricultural land, it can be quite a scary statement. Grassland is prone to many nasties, especially wireworms and leatherjackets. Neglected plots harbour many pests that have bred to infestation levels and 'Nearly' was home to a rampant colony of wireworms, but only in two of its four quarters, so over three years we'd had the unimaginable rollercoaster of one fantastic potato harvest between two rotten, worm-riddled ones.

The pestilential nature of well-established allotment sites had taught us to take nothing for granted. Now, if I visited the plot and found a new insect, blight or infestation, I reported to OH in shorthand.

'Another attack,' I would say.

'Bad?' If he'd been a flying ace in the Great War he'd have been twisting his moustache and 'reaching for the sky'.

There were three categories of attack: *bad*, *pretty bad* and *biblical*. *Biblical* meant that we were being visited with an infestation of plague proportions and was reserved for whitefly that could obscure an entire plant and cabbage white caterpillars when they ate a brassica down to the ribs. *Pretty bad* was losing half your crop, as in carrots to carrot fly. *Bad* was anything that could be classed as primarily cosmetic like the depredations of slugs on mature plants, although their habit of consuming seedlings down to ground level was definitely pestilential.

If nothing else, we'd toughened up over our years of allotment growing. I now squashed butterfly eyes with my bare thumb without a qualm, and OH had a nifty line in destroying whitefly with an evil-smelling spray composed of comfrey water in a mild saline solution.

The main problem with 'Nearly' was not the pests but us. We were just too impulsive, too inclined to find room for 'just one more' of something and too desperate to please the committee who were allowing us to manage the plot.

Part of the management deal was that we should grow an overstock of plants to distribute at low or no cost to new allotment-holders so that they had an instant range of crops to plant. That was easy when it came to tough and undemanding perennials like rhubarb and raspberries, but not so easy when we were raising tender annuals like sweet peppers and definitely difficult for the temperamental crops such as tomatoes and aubergines which were attractive to pests.

Growing overstocks to give away meant that we always had plants in pots or nursery beds, planted shallowly so they could be lifted to give to a new plot-holder. We wanted those plants to be impressive too, so we tended to give them high nitrogen feeds to make them big and shiny and green and sappy – and big sappy plants were a magnet for every kind of aphid and caterpillar, so we were always battling against some kind of invasion that tended to require non-organic treatments, which made the situation even worse.

If the plot had been our own, we would have lived with the problems, accepting wilted-looking plants, holes in leaves and so on, in favour of long-term treatments, but we felt compelled to give away only beautiful plants, so like insane plastic surgeons with body-dysmorphic clients we became ever more inclined to drastic measures. I wanted to be organic, and OH said he did too, apart from systemic weedkillers and anything he found in a spray in the garden centre that guaranteed to kill aphids. He sneaked such poisons on to the plot and I pretended not to notice, and we lived in an atmosphere of pest-hating collusion. Only rain put an end to our insane battles with insect life, and that was simply because the insects disappeared and left us to fight with the gastropods.

It was raining the morning of the farmers' market. Raining in bucket-loads, bathtub-loads even. I was fairly sure it wouldn't stop HSM: she was the type who would trek up Ben Nevis in a blizzard. I knew Celia would view the weather as a minor inconvenience at best, but I was worried that by the time she got there, other stall holders might have packed up because of the lack of trade, forcing HSM to do the same.

I was too nervous to do anything useful, so I spent the morning hovering near the house phone and clutching my mobile, waiting for Celia to call. By four in the afternoon I was fed up enough to have retreated to the garden and was bashing some old sunflower stalks with a rubber mallet to break them up before putting them in the compost bin.

The garden at home contained all the plants that couldn't be considered crops, plus a greenhouse and cold frame for hardening off seedling plants before taking them to the plot.

We had three compost bins on 'Nearly' and one at home and I was forever adjusting the proportions of waste (green, woody, swiftly-decomposing, fibrous and disgusting were the categories I used) to achieve the richest and most bulky compost possible to enrich our heavy clay soil. Stalk-smashing was a cathartic exercise that I tended to save for stressful periods like the week I had to send in my annual accounts, or the days following the sending out of cultivation notices, when furious allotment-holders ranted at me about being told their plot is not up to standard. So when Celia turned up, late in the afternoon, I was red-faced and sweating and wielding my mallet with berserk passion in the continuing drizzle. As usual, her calm elegance made me feel totally inadequate.

'Did you see her?' I asked.

Celia nodded and I could tell she was casting quick glances around the garden to see what I was growing and how tidy things were. Celia opened her garden for charity each year and her scrutiny was more pitying than judgemental but it made me feel acutely self-conscious. I needed to assert myself and I knew just how to do it.

'Come indoors and tell me what happened,' I said, leading the way.

Once we were settled in the kitchen, with tea and cake, I felt more equal. Celia was lovely, talented and a superb horticulturalist, but she couldn't cook.

'I'll cut a piece for you to take home for Stefan,' I said, holding my knife over the spiced apple cake. Celia nodded and waved the knife over until the portion was bigger. 'If he likes it I can give you the recipe,' I added wickedly.

Celia grimaced. Her reaction to my back garden was rather like mine when confronted with her kitchen. I had never seen evidence of a cake tin there, even saucepans huddled together in dusty corners, and I had a feeling that the oven door would screech like a Hammer Horror sound effect if anybody tried to open it.

I cut an even bigger slice. 'So?' I prompted.

Celia looked out of the window. 'There's something very odd going on with that woman,' she said.

'I know that.'

'No.' Celia shook her head. 'You're just thinking about the children, and I agree, their lives are a bit grey, but they are fed and taught and actually very much loved, so I think they will be fine. It's her I'm concerned about.'

I stayed silent. HSM as an object of sympathy was not what I'd been expecting.

'We had a chat, in fact I took her out for coffee while the children looked after the stall. I think she's being exploited by the HSF.'

I was reeling. 'Coffee? Exploited?'

Celia grinned. 'I had coffee, she had Fairtrade herbal tea. I admit I was quite worried that she might get down on her haunches and light a fire in the middle of the coffee shop to boil up a hedgerow tisane. She's quite... frugal.'

Frugal was definitely the word for it. 'So...' I said again, rather desperately.

'Before I go any further I want to check something. If she has the allotment, but *he* rents the market stall, is she actually breaking any rules?'

The way Celia said 'he' was disturbing, like hearing somebody else say 'monster' or 'vermin'.

I took my rulebook off the window sill. 'Rule 5.1 *Tenants must use their allotment for their own personal use and must not carry out any business or sell any produce from it, unless sold for the benefit of charity or the allotment association of that site,*' I read aloud. It was a rule that seemed to be getting a lot of attention recently.

'Bugger,' said Celia trenchantly. 'Then I'm not saying any more.'

'Oh come on, Celia! You can't just clam up. I'm not going to tell anybody anything.'

'Unless they ask you. I know you won't lie for her.'

'Who's going to ask me? It's an allotment committee, not the McCarthy hearings!'

Celia gave me another old-fashioned look. It seemed I had become a person who got looked at in one of two ways: old-fashioned or pitying. There had been a time in my life when people had looked at me with admiration, sometimes with flirtatious intent, but since I'd got 'nearly' a plot I had become a figure of scorn or derision. Perhaps I should start painting my fingernails again?

I looked at my hands and realised I'd have to grow some nails before I could paint them. Possibly it was already too late. I had inadvertently become a bag lady and the fact that the bag was bulging with home-grown vegetables only made it slightly less depressing. 'Awful but nutritious' was the sum of my current lifestyle estimation. It was time to do something about it, or I might start talking to myself and wearing a tea-cosy hat.

Celia patted my hand and I noticed that her elegant fingernails were beautifully manicured. 'You're like an assistant professor without tenure, my sweet. You depend on the committee for your very existence and so you are spineless. I don't want to take the risk that you might end up being cornered on the matter. Let me just say this: HSM is quite possibly deluded and HSF needs a talking to. Before the next farmers' market I intend to have a conversation with the absent father, and that could put me in a position to give you further information.'

I nodded, most of my attention having been diverted into wondering where the foot spa was. I knew we had one, but I hadn't seen it for several years. A pedicure, that was what I needed. And a haircut. And some good gardening gloves. And...

Celia took the cake and left, muttering about ordering a take-out for dinner (she and Stefan ordered in or ate out most nights of the week), and I began the quest for personal grooming items. By ten in the evening I had found a bottle of semi-congealed shocking pink nail varnish, some highly-scented bath salts that claimed to be gardenia but smelled more like a blend of DDT and candyfloss, and the foot spa, which had clearly been used as a propagator at some point in the distant past, as there were rings of potting compost indelibly engraved into its knobbly base. OH had rolled his eyes when I held up my battered hands with their broken nails and had taken the rest of the cake and a flask of tea off to the garage where he was doing something uncommunicative with power tools. The boy had wandered downstairs, looked at the nail varnish with mild interest, made a remark about anti-Goths and wandered off again.

I switched on the News at Ten, plugged in the spa, added water, poured in some bath salts and watched as an interesting blue spark travelled from the spa to the plug and shorted out the entire house.

Autumn Sensualities

There are few things more wonderful than autumn on an allotment. It's the time of year when the work rate slows but the rewards don't. The sun is warm and generous rather than scorching and the sounds are of contentment and relaxation: the birds have raised whatever young they can, and are no longer frantically screeching about every threat to their not-yet-fledged chicks; the fox cubs have been kicked out by their mum but are thriving on the autumn fruit, so they are big, replete and frisky; allotment-holders are enjoying the fruits, roots and leaves of their labours and smile at each other as they pass with wheelbarrows of manure or buckets of apples and pears.

Autumn is the best time of year for sensualists, and to be honest, if you're not a sensualist, you shouldn't have an allotment! Which is not to say that I think you should have to pass some kind of examination in earth-love and vegetable-worship: sensuality grows on most of us as we grow things in the ground. There's a tendency in modern life to remove us ever further from the original nature of things. The beaches we visit on holiday are bulldozed and cleaned at night, so they are smooth and clean the next day. The exercise we take in gyms simulates running and rowing and cycling, without ever exposing us to sun or rain, the scents carried on outdoor air or the insects and birds, animals and plants that we would pass if we undertook that exercise outside. The food we eat is packaged and pre-cooked so we never need to get our hands messy in creating it.

All this convenience is fantastic and often necessary, but it also denatures us and prevents us learning about our place in the world – our role in a complex and amazing eco-system on which we depend, but which also depends on us. Autumn is a great time to engage with the seasons, because as summer turns towards winter, we, in the kitchen, are able to hold back time, preserving the flavours, colours and tastes born of sunshine to release again in the short, dark, miserable days of winter.

If you have an allotment, autumn is when you need to drag out the list of jobs you can undertake indoors, because for periods of the season it's a waste of time to do anything that involves walking on the soil or digging it. When it rains, walking and digging compact the soil and damage its structure, unless you have very fine sandy soil, in which case ignore almost everything said in almost every gardening book about working with wet earth!

When it rains you can:

- Clean pots to use for next year's sowing

- Work out your crop rotation

- Clean and store onions, garlic and shallots you lifted earlier in the year

- Tidy the shed

🐝 Go home and make preserves

The reason I open-freeze a lot of my soft fruit and excess produce is that I want to use the good weather to be outdoors working my plot and still have something to do in the bad weather when I am marooned in the house. If you have enough space to freeze fruit and vegetables to use in preserves, it takes only a few minutes to wash and roughly pick over the produce, before drying it a little, putting it on trays (cheap plastic ones are fine) in a single layer and sliding it into the freezer. Next morning, tip the frozen fruit into a big resealable freezer bag and put it back in the freezer. I give this treatment to:

🐝 All berries

🐝 My courgette glut (washed, sliced and blanched for one minute in boiling water)

🐝 Excess French beans (you can use runners this way but you have to string them if they are at all elderly)

🐝 Cauliflower (broken into florets and blanched for two minutes)

Because I make jellies rather than jams, I don't need to worry too much about perfect preparation. The bits and pips stay in the jelly bag and as long as the fruit is clean and unblemished, I get perfect, translucent preserves from bags full of fruit (and the odd twig or leaf).

Vegetables require a little more care as food poisoning is possible if you don't bottle, preserve or 'chut' perfectly. After I'd read Carol Shields' novel, *Larry's Party*, in which

Larry's mother accidentally kills her own mother-in-law with inadequately preserved vegetables, I took down all my bottled green beans and threw them away, and have never bottled beans since!

The simplest recipes to get you started are chutneys, which are a bit like the vegetable soup of preserves: you can put a bit of almost anything in them and as long as you respect the three basic rules of chutney, you can't go wrong. Those rules are:

1. Cook your chutney long and slow until a wooden spoon scraped across the bottom of the pan leaves a clear line.

2. Use more spices than you think you need – people can always eat smaller quantities if the taste is robust, but they can't boost the flavour of an insipid condiment by eating more of it!

3. Keep it for six months before you try it. Many books say three months, but that's an absolute minimum, not a good average.

Making chutney is a good way to use up stored apples that have gone 'sleepy', which is just a way of saying they've begun to soften. It's generous enough to accommodate most glut vegetables and because it doesn't have to set, it's a great way to ease yourself into making preserves.

ALMOST INSTANT CHUTNEY

There is just one chutney recipe that I've found over the years that breaks the six-month rule. It's perfectly balanced between sweet and tart, and because it's cooked very slowly and thoroughly, the edge is taken off the vinegar and the colour is fully developed even before you pot it. I've eaten it a fortnight after making and found it to taste as good as most six-month chutneys.

To make this recipe you need a slow cooker. I can't recommend the slow cooker too highly as an aid to the time-poor allotment-holder, as it allows you to have a hot meal waiting for you when you get home from the plot. If you're cash-strapped, it can also be an economical way of making soups and stews, especially where they contain root vegetables that require protracted cooking times.

INGREDIENTS

- 1 kilogram apples, peeled, cored and roughly chopped – I use about half cookers and half eaters for extra sweetness
- 450 grams pears, peeled, cored and roughly chopped
- 225 grams onions, roughly chopped
- 500 grams dried fruit
- 4 cloves garlic, peeled
- 60 grams fresh ginger, peeled and chopped
- 1 fresh chilli, deseeded and chopped
- 1 lemon, quartered and with pips removed

- 15 grams grain mustard
- 600 ml malt vinegar
- 450 grams demerara sugar
- 15 grams black treacle
- 2 teaspoons salt

METHOD

Preheat the slow cooker according to manufacturer's instructions.

Put the apples, pears, onions, dried fruit, ginger, chilli and citrus fruit in a food processor and process briefly to make a coarsely chopped mixture. If you don't have a food processor, lay these ingredients out on a large chopping board and chop them all so that the biggest piece is about the size of a raisin.

Chuck into the slow cooker and add all the other ingredients apart from the vinegar.

In a microwave or saucepan heat the vinegar to boiling point, pour it over the rest of the ingredients and give them a good stir to blend. Leave to cook overnight or for at least eight hours. When it is soft, dark and wonderfully swampy, pour into a big pan (not a copper or aluminium one though, because those metals will react to the vinegar in dire ways) and cook over a medium heat for about twenty minutes, stirring regularly to stop it sticking on the bottom of the pan.

It is at this point that, according to Rule One of Chutney, you should be able to draw a line across the bottom of the pan and watch it fill in very, very, very slowly. This is only true if you have a pan the size of a circular bath. A better rule for small pans is to get a big metal spoon and press it down gently on the surface of the chutney. If liquid rushes into the bowl of the spoon, it's not cooked enough. If liquid seeps slowly over the sides of the spoon, your chutney is ready to pot.

Set your oven to 190°C (375°F) and preheat for about ten minutes. Then put your clean chutney jars upside down in the oven for five minutes to sterilise. Altogether your chutney will have been cooking in the pan for about thirty-five minutes at this point. Take the jars from the oven using gloves.

Using a jam funnel if you have one, or a large spoon with a non-heat-conducting handle if not, divide the chutney between the hot jars. The spoon will get very hot very quickly, which is why it needs to have a handle that doesn't transfer the heat to your fingers. Remember not to touch the jars too!

Depending on your jars, either screw non-metallic lids in place while hot or leave to cool and then seal with plastic pot covers. Once opened, store chutney in the refrigerator.

If you've got the hang of chutney and feel like expanding your preserving experience, a jelly is an impressive addition to your repertoire and only a little more complicated.

The key to making jam or jelly is pectin. Many fruits don't have enough pectin to set on their own, so you need to use added pectin to achieve set. Some fruits have an abundance of pectin and that means they set like rocks.

High pectin fruits suitable for jellying include: crab apples, gooseberries, plums, quinces and red, white and blackcurrants. Anything that's citrus has high pectin too.

CURRANT JELLY

This is delicious on toast, or in jam tarts, and if you enjoy rice puddings, it turns an average rice pudding into an absolute joy – simply plop a generous spoonful in the middle of each portion as you serve it up.

INGREDIENTS

- 1 kilogram redcurrants or mixed currants
- 500 grams sugar

UTENSILS

- A large wooden spoon
- A jelly bag or an old pillowcase that you won't be using again
- String
- Large bowl
- Sugar thermometer

PECTIN TEST KIT

- Two glass bowls or ramekins
- Methylated spirits

METHOD

Wash your fruit and take out any leaves and big woody stems.

Put the berries in a large saucepan, without water, and heat gently for around forty-five minutes. Stir every ten minutes or so.

Allow to cool a little before pouring the currants into your jelly bag or pillowcase. Hang the bag up to drip but don't squeeze it if you want translucent, glowing jelly. If, on the other hand, you don't care about the look of the thing, giving the bag a good pummelling every couple of hours can increase the juice production by nearly half.

Next morning, measure the extracted juice into a jug before returning it to the cleaned pan.

Put the sugar in a bowl and either heat it for ten minutes in a low oven, or two minutes on medium heat in the microwave. Warming the sugar means the jelly cooks quicker – the quicker it cooks, the fresher tasting the jelly will be.

Return the juice to the pan, add the right amount of sugar and bring to the boil, stirring gently.

Use the same system of warmed jars as you used for the chutney. At the instant the jelly boils, stop stirring, add the sugar thermometer to the pan and when it reaches 'jam' continue to boil for two minutes without stirring.

Do a quick pectin check: pour a teaspoon of jelly into one bowl, swirl to cool and then add a tablespoon of methylated spirits and leave for one minute. Pour the contents of one container gently into the other. If the pectin is low it will pour as threads, if it is medium level you will see clots of jelly and if it is high, one solid lump of jelly.

If the pan contains a white scum, drop a fragment of butter the size of a little fingernail into the jelly to break it down. Pour the jelly into the warmed jars swiftly and cover with a silicone circle. Dampen a cellophane jar topper and stretch it over the warm jar, securing it with a small elastic band.

An Inspector Calls

I was still in disgrace and hiding from OH as much as possible after the debacle with the foot spa. As a result, spending long hours out of the house was conducive to family harmony. Tracking down the reports of the South of England Show was easy enough; there were pages and pages of them. I tried to call Celia but, as usual, her mobile was switched off, so I trundled down to her plot with the reports in a carrier bag and Rebus trotting alongside me. Celia had requested his presence as a neighbouring cat was using her seed bed as a toilet and she hoped Rebus would widdle on enough posts and supports to make the feline think again.

When we got to the plot Celia wasn't around, so I sat down for a few minutes to let Rebus carry out his doggy tasks while I worked out what to do next. As usual, Celia's plot combined mystery with starkness. Her bare earth paths wove in and out of beds you needed a mastery of geometry to name: no squares or circles here, but rhombuses and unequal triangles, each carefully calculated to offer an evenly dappled shade or exactly the same amount of drainage or to fall under or avoid the shelter offered by a nearby structure so as to protect or expose the plants to the conditions most likely to cause them to thrive. It was a completely different kind of plot to 'Nearly' ours, which had serried ranks of potatoes and poles of beans, wigwams of sweet peas and well-stocked raised beds. I fondly imagined that ours resembled a Victorian kitchen garden, while hers looked more like the vegetative equivalent of Frankenstein's laboratory.

Today her plot held several glass bell cloches, which were a peculiarly malefic addition to the view. They had steamed up under the influence of the late afternoon sun and I itched to know what was hidden beneath, but I knew better than to lift them. They could be concealing anything from an edelweiss that needed daytime heat and night frost through to some arcane South American orchid that was only pollinated by a moth whose larvae Celia had placed under the cloche to avoid releasing a potential environmental hazard into our ecosystem.

Rebus cocked his leg with the kind of dedicated fussiness only a small terrier can bring to matters of the toilet while I took out the reports and started to read through them, determined to try to discover what Celia thought was hidden within them. I hit a problem immediately. The participants in the events and doings, shows, prizes, exhibitions and talks were all listed under title, initial and surname. Felix was a member of the association so I knew his surname: Sharpe. 'Sharpe by name

and sharp by nature,' Maisie said of him. But Maisie herself was not in the association so while I might find references to F. Sharpe (which had caused Celia to collapse in giggles the first time she saw it written down) I wasn't going to be able to identify Maisie if she was even mentioned, which I doubted. It didn't seem her kind of thing at all.

Rebus had run out of supplies and was performing air widdles – the canine equivalent of air kisses. 'You're ridiculous,' I said. He gave me a contemptuous glance and lay down doing his famous 'dog abandoned on allotment by unfeeling owner' impression.

I riffled through the reports, hoping something would leap out at me, and it did. A display of preserved fruits featured such exotic items as glacé greengages, crystallised golden raspberries and vinegar poached blueberries. Golden raspberries – the contentious fruit! Why were the fruits that caused discord always golden: the apples of the Hesperides, the Judgement of Paris, Iddun the Norse Goddess who had some golden apples and was kidnapped, apples and all, by an eagle...

I shook myself back to my detective work. The display had been created by a Miss L. Kerr, who could have been Felix's ex-girlfriend Lorna. So, preserved raspberries that would have been ripe in September, on show in a tent at the South of England Show in June. It sounded very clever, but how could it have caused a rift between Felix and Maisie?

Celia appeared, a small fair-haired figure, striding up the main path between the plots. Rebus saw her and sat up, wagging his tail uncertainly. I think he views Celia with the same blend of affection and nervousness as I do.

She took in the situation at a glance. 'Good dog,' she said and Rebus relaxed immediately.

'Worked it out?' she asked me, tapping the report.

'It's definitely something to do with the raspberries,' I said. 'But I don't know what.'

Celia peered at the text and tapped a line at the bottom of the page. 'Miss L. Kerr's display fruits courtesy of F. Sharpe,' she read aloud, trying to suppress her mirth.

'So Felix got the credit and Maisie didn't, but I still don't see why she would get so upset,' I said. And then I did see, dimly, through some almost forgotten conversation which had revealed that Maisie, like the Wickendens, Ansells and Baxters, came from an ancient local line. 'Maisie's a Stoneham! Her maiden name, I mean. One of the committee told me that because years ago her dad was the Jack Stoneham who won an RHS medal for his allotment. And…' I was riffling through the report manically now, trying to find the right paragraph. 'Yes! Miss L. Kerr was displaying her skills in the—'

'Archibald Stoneham Marquee,' Celia said smugly. 'I've given presentations there myself, on the role of climate change in domestic vine-fruit growing.'

'Sounds riveting,' I muttered, then added, a bit louder: 'But what about Maisie and Felix and Miss L. Kerr?'

Celia frowned. 'I think it all went something like this: Archibald Stoneham left a bequest to establish a section of the show devoted to fruit. Jack Stoneham was probably his son or grandson, and Maisie, as we know, was very proud of her dad and his RHS medal. So when she saw Miss L. Kerr's display, featuring fruit she recognised as her late dad's own unique variety of golden raspberries, she probably expected Jack to get a nice acknowledgement. But no. It was her dubious allotment-neighbour Felix who was thanked and…'

Celia was warming to her task and Rebus and I leaned forward as she dropped her voice. 'Maisie is a proud person. She probably didn't make a fuss at the time, but she'd have sped back to the allotment, maybe even under cover of darkness and searched out the suckering canes that Felix had urged to take root on his side of the boundary.'

I took up the tale, Rebus's head swinging towards me like that of a spectator at a tennis match.

'Armed with her evidence, she'd have gone to the committee, but somehow Felix wriggled off the hook. Maybe he claimed innocence or maybe he said she'd given him permission to take cuttings. Either way, it was her word against his.'

'And we know what the committee was like in the old days,' Celia interrupted me. 'Rude and chauvinistic and not likely to take Maisie's side.'

'But she's not the kind to give up easily,' I grabbed the story back. 'So she confronted Lorna, telling her how Felix had stolen the raspberries and deprived poor Jack of his moment of glory in the family tent.' I paused for breath, which was a mistake, as Celia leapt in. Poor Rebus was starting to look a little dizzy.

'And Lorna, shocked to discover how duplicitous her lover was, or maybe having had her darker suspicions about the untrustworthy Felix confirmed, left.'

'So the feud was established,' I raised my voice, determined to have the last word. 'Felix blames Maisie for the loss of his sweetheart and Maisie blames Felix for stealing Jack's thunder.'

We grinned at each other, not sure if we'd found *the* truth, but certain we'd found a good truth, one that fitted the personalities involved and gave colour to our sometimes dour allotment life.

'Anyway, I'm surprised you're here,' said Celia. 'Are you hiding?'

There was only one thing that could make me hide – publication of the results of the Jubilee Cup: a hotly-contested local award for the best allotment.

'Jubilee Cup is over for the year,' I said, and watched Celia raise her eyebrows. I backtracked frantically and remembered that today was inspection day.

Inspection day, and I hadn't been to my plot to check that everything was as perfect as possible! In fact, with the rain and fruit falling from the pear tree that our neighbour allowed to expand over our boundary, and the investigations into various allotment mysteries that had taken up a lot of my time recently, 'Nearly' could be looking distinctly tatty.

In one way it didn't matter. In another it mattered very much indeed.

As Celia had waspishly pointed out, I was at the mercy of the committee and if I didn't keep them happy, I could lose my plot in an instant. Conversely, as long as I pleased the committee, I probably didn't have to worry about inspection.

Everybody knew I was allotment secretary. 'Nearly' our plot was a corner one, near an entrance gate, which meant that around a quarter of those who visited the allotment came past it. Our progress, or lack of it, was commented on in public and private. Sometimes, given the age of allotment-holders, comments were meant to be private but the volume necessary to get their views into the ears of their elderly companions meant the result was very public indeed. It was in this way that I had discovered that Betty and Reg, who had a plot diagonally opposite ours, thought it was 'a crying shame' that OH and I had 'pruned the life out of that lovely old currant' and that Brian, who'd been on the committee thirty-five years ago, agreed with them that our organic nonsense was going to end in tears.

It was important to me to show that I respected the best of the old ways, without being a slave to them. Our outward-leaning bean poles had caused many a chortle until I demonstrated that you could harvest an entire row of runner beans in a tenth of the time it took to find and pick the same amount of beans on a wigwam. Our experiment with three ways of planting leeks had been a topic of intense debate and several of the old guard had come along to examine the relative girth, weight and quality of produce from the three beds.

In short, I had a reputation to maintain, and it wasn't for the quality of my sentences. 'Where did they start?' I asked urgently.

'South-east corner,' Celia replied. 'I saw them with their clipboards when I was buying blood, fish and bone in the shop.'

I had time! I grabbed my bag and set off at a run, almost tugging Rebus off his feet.

Once on 'Nearly' I swiftly washed down the brick path with water and brushed it with a stiff broom, then grabbed a pair of shears and took the heads off a couple of dandelions, trimmed the sage and the bay tree so they looked manicured, and just managed to shove the trimmings, plus the fallen pears, into the compost bins before the inspection group appeared in view, at which point I casually sauntered to the back of my plot and pretended I was wiring up the tendrils of my achocha vine.

I was proud of the achocha and wanted an opportunity to point out to the council allotment officer that it was a crop (South American, something like a midget cucumber in shape and between a green pepper and a pea pod in flavour) and therefore counted towards our cultivation proportion, rather than being purely ornamental like the passion flower which so many allotment-holders grew, but which had inedible fruits.

The inspectors passed without pausing to speak to me and I sighed with a combination of relief and annoyance: glad that they hadn't found anything they needed to confront me about but irritated that I hadn't been able to show off about my prize crop. We were safe for another quarter.

How to Win Inspections and
Impress Allotment Officers

Inspection is a complicated issue. For those who have an allotment it's like being stood over by a warder as you work. For those who don't have an allotment, inspection seems to be a system that fails to get to grips with plots that are lying weedy and neglected while the waiting list gets ever longer. For inspectors it is often a thankless task: never getting any thanks for the hours spent trudging around an allotment site, trying to work out whether a plot is in sixty or seventy-five per cent cultivation, or if the plot-holder can be allowed to claim that their raspberry thicket and Jerusalem artichoke jungle are crops rather than invasive plants run riot and being lambasted by allotment-holders who've been issued a 'notice' they don't think they deserve.

Inspection used to be a low-key affair, almost non-existent during the 1970s and 1980s, when sites struggled to get allotment-holders at all. Maisie could remember the days when allotment-holders on our site played impromptu cricket matches on the expanses of unworked land that had been allowed to revert to grass dotted with random fruit trees that made life interesting for the outfield.

It was easy to think that our huge and popular allotment community was invulnerable, but it was less than a decade since another, equally large and popular, allotment site had been turned into a hospital, all the tenants being offered allotments elsewhere in the city. That our site was still intact was partly due to the stubborn persistence of the old codgers who'd maintained the plots and they were not inclined to give up their rambling allotments, with half a dozen sheds, complicated water-storage systems and areas given over to outdoor dining, ranks of drying racks for onions and corrugated plastic carports, amongst other oddities! Maisie's father had taken on four consecutive allotments and kept them in nominal order by borrowing the gang mower used on the nearby playing fields. In fact we still had several allotment-holders who had occupancy of three or more plots, and it was an impossible issue to resolve: if the plots were in good order, it seemed unfair to take them away, but however well maintained they were, it was also unfair for one person to have four when others had none.

The first rule of inspection is to read the rules. Understanding what's important on your allotment site stops you becoming complacent about your tenancy. Our own committee had endured a couple of run-ins with 'wildlife gardeners' whose plots no longer met the cultivation standards of the most recently issued rules. Such allotment-holders were vociferous about their right to maintain what they called a 'leisure garden' as described in the 1922 Act of Parliament. They didn't want to hear that the rules, and the world, had changed and that the British public had rediscovered the fun of, and in some cases the necessity for, home-grown food.

Cash-strapped, time-rich, recently-made-redundant folk eyed the 'leisure gardens' hungrily, and lashed out in the local press, complaining that they 'couldn't afford to feed their families while so-called allotment-holders planted wildflower meadows that anybody else would call weeds'. Inspections, in recession-hit times, are often bitter affairs. And our city council had just caused great unrest in the allotment world, making passing inspections even more important.

They had sent letters to everybody on the allotment waiting list, asking if they wanted to remain on the list or be removed. This had churned up long-dormant and murky antagonisms. The allotment community, normally fairly serene, had divided implacably into two groups: 'real' allotment-holders like Maisie, Felix, Chaz and HSM, and the rest of us, who'd taken on somebody else's plot – as co-workers, plot-sitters and volunteers – whilst waiting to reach the top of the list.

'Real' allotment-holders couldn't see what the fuss was about and felt as if the rest of us were ill-wishing them so we could 'steal' their plots. 'The rest of us', myself included, were suddenly aware that we might never get a plot of our own. The council's attempt to shorten the list by removing anybody who didn't reply within thirty days had an unexpected side effect – list members started talking to each other about how long they'd been waiting and how much land the 'real' allotment-holders actually possessed. Chaz became a haunted figure. His four plots were contiguous and near the main gate, so it was obvious one man was running them all. Like the sans-culottes outside Versailles, would-be allotment-holders pressed their noses to the railings around our site and bayed hungrily.

I had a nasty shock when I went to the office to examine the current waiting list: something I'd never bothered to do before. There were people ahead of me in the queue that I knew had signed up several years after me! The committee couldn't explain the discrepancy and when I rang the council they had no idea why I'd slipped down the list, nor any interest in putting things right. Eventually, by picking out names on the list that I recognised and finding out when they thought they'd signed up compared to where they appeared in the queue, I worked out that a previous allotment officer had either lost or failed to register several years of co-worker forms.

These forms allowed co-workers to receive a key to the allotment gates and registered their interest in the plot they were helping to cultivate: if the plot-holder gave up their tenancy the council could, if it wished, give the co-worker first refusal on the plot. A co-worker could also choose to be on the allotment waiting list. I had registered as a co-worker on a different allotment site in the city back in the late 1990s, but my name didn't appear on the list with other 1998 registrants. Instead I appeared somewhere around the 2005 mark. Given that the waiting list was over a decade long, I was furious.

Rachel was even more furious – her name wasn't on the list at all! She brought Lola to my plot and I made us tea while Rachel let off steam at about the same rate as my storm kettle.

'I'll never get a plot,' she hissed, attacking with her pocket knife the dandelions I'd beheaded a few days earlier.

I watched warily. An unbalanced woman with a knife was a fairly disturbing companion on a largely deserted allotment site.

'I thought it *was* your plot?'

She shook her head silently. Lola and Rebus sat together in the weak sunshine, Lola prattling away and Rebus pretending polite interest. 'When did you sign up then?'

'2002. Year we got married. Bastards!' The epithet could have been for the council or the weeds and I decided not to seek clarification which.

'So whose plot is it?'

'Steve's mum's.' Her bitterness was palpable – I was surprised the dandelions didn't wilt under it.

'The Waitrose Woman?'

Rachel nodded. The Waitrose Woman visited the plot once a year at strawberry time, when she picked and packed strawberries, patronised the rest of us and ensured Steve spent the next few weekends tracking down and apologising to anybody he thought she might have offended. I'd heard her describe me, in carrying tones, as 'Looking like a gypsy. And not...' she'd added, 'in a nice way. There's something of the lurcher about her.'

I could understand Rachel's fury. Being grateful to the Waitrose Woman would only be endurable if you knew that one day you'd be free of her.

'I rang the council when I didn't get a letter.' As she spoke Rachel was excavating a dandelion root with cold, deliberate venom. The opportunistic part of me wondered if I could move her on to a persistent clump of thistles near the compost bins. 'They said there was no record of my co-worker form.'

'Have you signed up now?'

She nodded, but we both knew that the current interest in allotments meant she'd be lucky to be offered a plot before Lola left home for university. We drank our tea silently and Rachel headed back to the plot I'd always thought was hers. 'It's a good thing we're organic,' she said as she left. 'Or I'd probably put weedkiller in her Pinot Grigio, just to get a shot at the tenancy.'

I nodded my understanding. It might seem trivial to people outside our community of growers, but we'd invested time, money and emotions in the land we worked. It was infuriating to discover an inept bureaucracy had damaged our chances of ever becoming legal tenants of the plots we loved.

I sent back my letter saying I wanted to stay on the list and forgot about it. Sometimes I would hear other co-workers talking about 'the list' and I knew that my position as secretary would allow me to see our site's list whenever I liked, but it was a dubious privilege and after a single question to ensure I was actually still on it, I chose not to check. It was better to live in hope than face the potential disappointment of reality.

 ## Top Ten Inspection Tips

1. Cultivated area – on my site, this has become the most argued point of contention when an inspection is carried out. The old term of 'good order' no longer applies and where it used to be enough to have a tidy plot, pretty well whether or not you were growing anything, today each plot has to meet a minimum percentage of cultivation (rule 2.1 *Cultivation requires the tenant to regularly dig or mulch, or prune and weed 75% of the plot*) and the items that are included in your cultivated area can vary from site to site, even within the same local authority.

2. Weeds – perennial weeds are easy to spot and bloody annoying to your neighbours. If an inspection is due and you really don't have time to weed, get in there with a strimmer or shears and take the

flowering heads off thistles, dandelions and bindweed because those flowers scream 'neglect' to an inspector. Removing the flowering heads shows that you at least understand that it's your responsibility to protect your neighbours from weed invasion. Weedy plots, in most places, get issued a weed or cultivation notice. Failure to improve the situation in the time stipulated in the notice usually means termination of tenancy.

3. Structures – again, allowable structures vary from site to site. Plot terminations have been issued to tenants for having boats on their plots (not because of the boat but because of the paved area on which it stood), for using concrete footings and even using a shed as a pirate radio station! Our local authority has just thrown an interesting new rule into the mix (rule 8.5 *Any structures erected on the allotment shall not be made from hazardous materials and the colour shall be in keeping with the natural environment*) which is likely to create some arguments in the months ahead. Is pink in keeping with the natural environment? What about yellow? At least three sheds on our plot are made of bright yellow plastic and were purchased in an auction of ex-council equipment more than a decade ago. I don't fancy being in the inspection team that decides they have to be painted or removed.

4. Rubbish – most sites give you a period of time after taking over a plot to clear rubbish. Again your little book of rules will tell you if you have to dispose of it, if the council will clear it, or if you put the rubbish

in a marked area that gets emptied by contractors. Some sites have skips and some have wardens: there are as many ways of dealing with rubbish as there are of creating it. Allotment-holders need to be sure they understand what counts as rubbish and what doesn't and what you get charged for. Some councils are now levying a charge for clearing overgrown plots and they aren't necessarily giving the tenant advance warning that their plot is being cleared and they are going to be billed for the work.

5. Bonfires – the rules are strict. Know yours well. Whatever the rules, be a sensible fire-starter not an insane pyromaniac. Fireworks are banned on a lot of sites – find out what the rules are on your site before you decide to have a Guy Fawkes party because in recent years there have been immediate terminations following Firework Night complaints by residents living near allotment sites.

6. Paths – paths of certain dimensions are allowed. Exceeding those dimensions will normally mean that the path isn't included in the cultivated area (see Tip 1). There have been cases in different parts of the country where plot-holders have had their tenancies terminated for having double-width gravel paths, for failing to maintain their side of a shared path and for dumping rubbish on access roads.

7. Ponds – hedges and ponds have become almost as contentious as percentages of cultivation. We have the confusing rule 4.7 *The use of sunken baths as*

ponds or for water storage is not permitted on safety grounds. Baths being brought onto the allotment space by an existing tenant will be seen as unwanted waste and will result in a tenant being put on notice. Historical baths brought on-site before the 2010 rule review that are both functional and above ground will be exempt. That presumably means that non-existing tenants can bring as many baths as they like and that there is something called wanted waste, as opposed to the unwanted kind. This kind of rule can cause an allotment committee to resign en masse. It also causes tenants to lose their tenancies: if you're in doubt, ask the council allotment officer for a written ruling and demand a reasonable deadline if the decision is that you must remove a pond or water storage system – ninety days is quite common for such a deadline.

8. Immorality – it's illegal. Despite the *Darling Buds of May* effect (which means that anybody near gooseberry bushes or a man whose trousers are held up with string immediately becomes robustly suggestive in the Pa Larkin style), using your plot for illegal, immoral or antisocial purposes will – almost everywhere – get your tenancy terminated immediately. On allotment sites owned by the Church of England there can be some odd little rules about Sunday working, which comes under immoral behaviour, believe it or not, but I don't think they are enforced any more. Anyway, I doubt that many people are unlucky enough to get caught being immoral during a site inspection.

9. Unwelcome visitors – anything from noisy parties through to invasive plants can lead to termination of tenancy. Most sites now have rules about the height of fruit trees, some have rules about what can and can't be grown in terms of perennial plants (Giant hogweed, Japanese knotweed and *Gunnera manicuta* are all outlawed on different sites around the UK). Sleeping on your plot overnight is forbidden almost everywhere these days and on some sites you're not allowed to leave your car on-site overnight either. I'm wondering if ours is the only council to have made specific mention of yurts! (Rule 15.2 *Overnight erection of tents, yurts and other temporary structures, as well as overnight camping, are not allowed on allotment land.*)

10. Dogs, livestock and bees – rules vary. Some councils allow bees but individual sites sometimes don't; beekeeping is becoming increasingly controversial. Many plot-holders are keen to promote healthy bee populations for biodiversity and pollination reasons; others are just as keen to avoid hive bees because they, or members of their family, suffer from bee sting allergy which can be life-threatening. I don't think chickens are life-threatening, but many sites don't allow poultry-keeping. Photos of allotment sites before World War Two usually show at least a few pigeon-lofts, but I haven't seen anybody keeping pigeons on an allotment site for many years and I'm not sure that councils would allow it now for health and safety reasons. Dogs should be kept on leads on

almost every allotment site whose rules I've seen and on some sites you are not allowed to have a dog on your plot unless the plot is fenced.

If You Like Astringency...

The fruits and vegetables that have a predominantly bitter or astringent taste are the ones that most people list as their 'hates'. In this class I would put rhubarb and gooseberry and the chicory family (especially radicchio) but not the brassicas which are also top of the 'hate' list but cause pained expressions for a different reason.

Tolerance for brassicas (cabbages, broccoli, Brussels sprouts, etc.) comes from our genes. A certain class of people, called 'supertasters', are sensitive to a particularly bitter chemical compound – 6-n-propylthiouracil, familiarly known as PROP – which they find unpalatably strong. Some people, known as 'non-tasters', just don't pick up any taste of PROP at all, while 'medium tasters' do get the bitterness on their taste buds but don't object to it.

Virtually all children, pre-puberty, have a stronger reaction to PROP than adults, so the childhood hatred of 'greens' is not just picky eating, and may fade by one's twenties, which suggests that this supertaster gene may be an evolutionary mechanism that stopped primitive children eating unsafe foods as they foraged alongside adults. The diminishing response to PROP makes perfect sense if this instinctive response was replaced by learning what foods were safe as the child grew. It also proves that the parent who tries to force their offspring to eat their 'lovely, healthy greens' is on a hiding to nothing. Much better to wait until the kids grow up and give them another chance to try their PROP reactions. In my family both my parents love brassicas, as do I, but my brother is a supertaster and wouldn't eat them until he was in his thirties. OH is also a brassica-lover but our son has never knowingly eaten one and we are hoping that when he gets to adulthood his tastebuds will relent and allow him to enjoy what the rest of us adore.

Back to astringents. These are not necessarily foods that are PROP-rich. Rhubarb and gooseberries tend to be a little tongue-puckering regardless of how much sugar you add to them, and their mouth-watering astringency might indicate health benefits, as they encourage saliva production which is essential for good digestion. Rhubarb, in particular, is remembered with scorn and loathing by many who had it inflicted on them as part of school dinners served up as an unappetising, stringy, grey-green mess, swimming with unnaturally yellow custard which the rhubarb juice would cut into vile-looking curds.

This is tragic, as rhubarb can be utterly delicious, and is at its best when baked, rather than boiled, and served with strawberries, which are in season around the same time and whose sweet denseness provides a natural complement to rhubarb's juicy astringency.

Rhubarb has many advantages, not least that it is easy to grow. If the planet is side-swiped by a nuclear disaster, I predict that along with the cockroaches, rhubarb plants will survive! However, just because it will cope with neglect, that doesn't mean rhubarb should be ignored. You can grow rhubarb as sweet and tender as a peach, if you're prepared to put in a bit of effort. It's called champagne or forced rhubarb, and it's just about the first fresh fruit of the year.

To grow a champagne rhubarb, lift a rhubarb crown in November, replant it in a big black pot in pure compost and put it in the shed (mild winter expected) or the spare bedroom (harsh winter expected) on a watering tray and covered with an inverted black bin.

A champagne rhubarb needs to be watered every couple of weeks through the winter and kept in total darkness. It will then produce finger-thick, fondant-pink and apple-green stems at around the same time that canny gardeners will be covering their outdoor rhubarb to force the stems that are just beginning to shoot. We do this every year and there is no limit to the smugness we feel when we're eating our first rhubarb just as other folk are beginning to think about forcing theirs!

Once harvested – and you only get one cutting of champagne rhubarb – we replant the crown, usually next to the compost bins, and ignore it for the next two years to allow it to rebuild its strength. If you try to harvest off a forced crown within twelve months it's likely to die of exhaustion. As we don't cut stems from a forced crown for a couple of years, it can happily sit near the compost, feeding itself up on the runoff from the bins, and then we'll move it back into the rhubarb bed in year three – taking out another crown to force and slotting the well-rested one into the vacant place.

But it's the classic outdoor rhubarb that works best with strawberries because you harvest the last of the rhubarb in late June or July just as the strawberries ripen enough to be picked.

The following recipe will win over any reluctant rhubarb eater. It's not a pretty dessert, so if you like food that looks dainty it may not impress you until you taste it, but the combination of piquant rhubarb with sweet strawberries, lifted by the zing of the orange, makes up for any lack of elegance in appearance!

SUMMER FRUITS SPONGE

INGREDIENTS

- 6 sticks rhubarb, cut into two-centimetre pieces (no need to peel)
- 250 grams strawberries (use whole ones if they are small, or hull and halve large ones)
- 250 grams caster sugar in two 125 gram batches
- 75 grams butter or margarine
- 1 egg
- 2 teaspoons grated orange zest
- 1 teaspoon vanilla extract
- 150 grams flour
- 1 teaspoon baking powder
- 160 ml milk

METHOD

Preheat the oven to 180°C (360°F) and grease a twenty-three centimetre baking dish – if it has low sides, you may need to put some greaseproof paper around them to ensure the sponge can rise properly.

Put the rhubarb, strawberries and 125 grams of sugar in a plastic bag and shake well to coat, then pour the whole mixture into the greased dish and spread it out so it forms an even layer over the bottom.

Beat the rest of the sugar and the butter together, then add the egg, orange zest and vanilla. When the mixture is well combined, begin to add the flour, mixed with the baking powder, alternating big spoonfuls of flour with sloshes of milk to form a wet batter which you pour gently over the fruit. Don't let the batter push all the fruit down to one end of the dish, as that's disappointing for the person who gets no fruit in their portion!

Bake for around 55 minutes or until a skewer inserted into the centre comes out clean.

If you like astringency in food, and enjoy having your taste buds titillated, then the radicchio di Treviso may be your winter vegetable of choice. However, it's not a beginner's plant, unless you're prepared for disappointment, so it may be best to get a year of growing under your belt before you take it on.

First things first: Treviso is a different beast to the radicchio that you get in bags of supermarket salad. It's much more upright in growth, hearts up to form a furled inner core, and has a tough stalk that supports it through the colder weeks of the autumn and winter. It's also usually sown where it grows, as transplants will tend to bolt even in winter. Above all, it really doesn't like warmth.

To grow it, sow directly into prepared ground around four weeks before the expected first frost. Once the seedlings are a couple of inches tall, mulch around them to hold moisture and suppress late weeds. Don't over-protect from weather – the cold serves to mellow the flavour and the outer leaves act as a blanching jacket for the inner ones: in Veneto, where it is grown in kitchen gardens, they say the colder the weather, the sweeter the radicchio!

Once you've harvested a crown, cover the stump with a mulch of leaves or grass clippings and you may find you get a tiny, tightly-furled crimson second crop, harvestable around February. These are delicious sliced lengthways into quarters and roasted with sweeter vegetables – just add them fifteen minutes before the end of cooking time to a dish of roast potatoes or parsnips, sprinkling them with olive oil before you drop them in the roasting pan and topping with a little grated parmesan just before you serve. They add a tang to the earthy root vegetables which is very palate-cleansing.

For larger crowns, and for those who aren't sure they want to live dangerously, a marinade can make the astringency piquant rather than tongue-curling.

BAKED RADICCHIO DI TREVISO

Allow half a crown per person, and after removing the outer leaves, which are often brown if they have been caught by frost, slice the crown in half lengthways and then marinate in a mixture of olive oil, salt and pepper for around ten minutes. I don't know why this works, and perhaps you'd have to be Heston Blumenthal to find out, but all the books say that an oil marinade takes some of the bitterness out of radicchio and I've found it to be true. Marinate is perhaps not the best word – just whisk some seasoning in with a couple of tablespoons of oil and then brush it over the uncut side of the halved crown before turning it over in your hand, dobbing the oil into the crevices on the cut side and leaving it cut side up for the oil to trickle down inside for a few minutes.

INGREDIENTS

- 2 eggs
- 75 ml single cream
- 60 grams grated Taleggio cheese (if you have a good Italian delicatessen nearby, you might find Scamorza which is a smoked mozzarella – it's the gourmet choice for this dish, but Taleggio is good too)
- 60 grams grated Parmesan
- 4 slices prosciutto (vegetarians may like to use several slices of grilled red pepper instead)
- 75 ml olive oil

METHOD

Preheat the oven to 190°C (375°F) while you marinate the radicchio and beat the eggs, cream and Taleggio together in a bowl. Take each half of radicchio and place it with the cut side down in a shallow greased baking dish, before topping it with the slices of prosciutto or pepper. Pour the cheese mixture over the vegetable and then sprinkle the whole with the Parmesan cheese. Bake until the egg and cheese mixture sets, which will take around 15 minutes.

This is a good side vegetable for fatty meats or makes a great simple lunch when served with thinly-sliced crusty bread.

When Did You Last See Your Father?

When the committee had offered us 'Nearly' I had seen all the advantages and none of the disadvantages. The brick path and the pretty shed, somewhat like a Swiss chalet, had blinded me to other features, as had the chest-high weeds. When we hacked down the forest of thistles and raspberries run wild we found a cold frame the size of a small car – quite a hidden bonus!

But there were nasty surprises too: 'Nearly' our plot was on a corner with low pallet fences and no screening so when I was on the plot I could be seen from several hundred yards away. This was convenient for association members, who didn't have to traipse all the way to the plot to see whether I was 'at home' to visitors, but less convenient for me, as I couldn't avoid some of the more negative or difficult members. After several weeks of hearing about one allotment-holder's bunions, OH took to hopping over the back fence and going to visit Chaz whenever our ill-footed neighbour appeared.

Being near a gate was both good and bad. It meant we didn't have to walk far with our harvested crops but also that everybody else found it convenient to take a breather when they got to us, so our allotment work was constantly interrupted by arrivers and departers who who'd pause to compare our crops to their own, usually to our detriment. Generally speaking, 'Nearly' our plot's location gave me a snapshot of activities on the site, so when I hadn't seen HSM for a few days, I became concerned.

Her absence, on bright but chilly autumn days, was disturbing. Most allotment-holders were getting to the plot whenever they could, snatching time in a lunch-break or grabbing a few minutes before it got dark, to complete the tasks it would be horrible to undertake in winter. HSM would normally have been foremost in clearing the shading from her greenhouse, mouse-proofing stored seeds and taking home the onions and garlic she'd dried on her shed roof for use through the winter.

When I got to her plot, with its abundant native hedging, I was confronted by a large and well-padlocked gate. HSM had never been secretive. She'd tried to keep Portia, Reatta and Ayar away from what she saw as negative influences, but she was generous with her knowledge and always on hand to offer an organic solution to a crop problem. This new isolationist behaviour puzzled and worried me. I rattled the gate as a gesture of frustration and to my astonishment Ayar's head appeared through a knee-high gap in the hedge.

'Are you locked in?' I asked, hardly a sensible question as I could see the padlock in front of me.

Ayar looked as if he was about to cry. 'I'm not asposed to tell you.'

There was a rapid movement of leaves and he disappeared, to be replaced by Portia. I was more than a little amused to realise that an ancient metaphor had just been brought to life before my eyes, but Ayar's sobs from inside the hedge brought me back to reality. Something was very wrong here.

I squatted down so that Portia didn't have to twist her neck to see me.

'What's going on?' I asked. 'Is your mum there?'

Portia shook her head.

'Well that's a problem. I think you should all crawl out of that hole and come to my allotment. We can leave a note for your mother, so she can come and collect you.'

There was a muffled exclamation from beyond the hedge, in which I could only make out the word 'cake' in Ayar's squeaky tones. Portia shook her head. 'We're OK,' she said.

They so clearly weren't OK that I felt a fury at HSM and her crackpot ways that should have blown the padlock right off its hasp. 'I'm sorry Portia, but that's not good enough. I can't think, off the top of my head, what allotment rule your mother is breaking, but she certainly isn't taking proper care of you by locking you in there.'

Portia's head swivelled left and right as she checked we were alone. 'We're not really locked in,' she said. 'We can get out the back as easy as anything. It's just a ruse.'

The way she said 'ruse' suggested the word was new to her, and rather exciting.

'What kind of ruse?' I was intrigued.

Portia shook her disembodied head. 'Don't know. It's all right though, your friend knows – she helped Mum choose the gate.'

'My friend?'

Portia nodded. 'The clever one.'

That could only be Celia. I took pride in my own intellect but 'clever' in HSM terms meant horticultural intelligence and there, compared to Celia, I was a grinning fool.

'So where's your mother?' I asked.

Portia shook her head, either not knowing or not willing to say.

'Well, we have a choice. You can stay in there and I'll call the police, or you can sneak out through whatever secret passageway you use and be on my plot in ten minutes. Understood?'

She nodded and I walked away, wanting them to know I wasn't trying to find their route in and out. I had no idea what was going on, but they had to be feeling pretty insecure so I didn't want to remove whatever little confidence they had in their escape route.

I called Celia as I walked back but the phone went straight to voicemail. 'I have three visitors on my plot, who would like to be reunited with a person whom you seem to be popular with at present...' I was talking like a spy on a covert operation; this secrecy stuff must be infectious! 'So please convey that message if you have the opportunity.'

An hour or so later Celia appeared, her blonde head distinctive in the distance, accompanied by a grey figure that could only be HSM. Celia sent the children running up to their mother who had not walked down to 'Nearly'. 'Janice says thank you for looking after the children,' Celia said.

'Janice? She's called Janice?' It was just about the last name I'd have expected, seeming far too frivolous for the gaunt and humourless HSM. 'And what the hell is going on, anyway?'

Celia frowned. 'I can't tell you yet. Trust me when I say the children are safe and we wouldn't have left them on the plot unless we had to. There's a good reason they couldn't be at home or with us this afternoon. It will all become clear very soon.'

It became a bit clearer within twenty-four hours. I'd gone back up to 'Nearly' to finish the work I hadn't completed because I was entertaining the children, although I had a sneaking feeling they could have planted my broad beans better than I could myself.

Rebus and I were walking back down to the gate in the dusk when we saw a figure lurking outside. I wasn't worried, as it was common to find allotment-holders faffing around in the winter months when darkness made locating the gate lock almost impossible and holding a torch, a key and a padlock simultaneously tested the patience of even the most tranquil individual.

As I got closer I made out a leather jacket the colour of a butternut squash, expensive black wool trousers, shiny boots and an extremely well-barbered head. Not anybody I knew, and definitely not one of us. I unlocked the gate and was immediately accosted by the man. 'I'm looking for my wife and children. I think they have an allotment here. Janice Westall, do you know her?'

I took my time answering, gazing at the elegance of the man I assumed must be HSF. He was certainly worth looking at! He knew it too, and gave me a smile that revealed his brilliant white teeth and his expectation that I would do whatever I could to assist him. For a moment I smiled back, basking in his presence, and then I remembered Portia, Reatta and Ayar in their grey clothing, and HSM's sombre appearance, and wondered why HSF wasn't sure where his wife had an allotment, when it took up so much of her time. Rebus ignored HSF, never a good sign in a dog whose default mode was to greet visitors politely, even cats.

I turned and locked the gate behind me, playing for time.

'It doesn't sound familiar,' I said – not entirely a lie: I'd been calling her HSM since I met her so her real name was quite unfamiliar to me. 'Why would they be here at this time of day?'

HSF looked around at the gathering gloom and shrugged. 'I don't know. They aren't at home and this was the only other place I could think of.'

I was rapidly going off HSF, despite his gorgeous hair and soulful brown eyes. I understood why Maisie had given me that old-fashioned look when I mentioned him: it was odd to look at such a gorgeous man and have such a feeling of distaste. 'Maybe your wife is visiting friends?'

'No,' he sounded definite. 'She doesn't have any friends.'

That did it. A man who could say his wife had no friends struck me as a pretty dire specimen, and the gap between his lush clothing and his family's poverty was too much for me to accept.

'You might be surprised about that,' I said. 'And if you continue to hang around here I shall call the police. We've had a series of attempted break-ins recently and you might be—'

But he'd gone before I got to the end of my sentence, his glossy boots striking the pavement hard as he strode away.

'… involved.' I finished, speaking to empty air. Well, that was odd: he'd almost run when I mentioned the police. Rebus and I walked home, wondering what that had been about. I tried calling Celia but once again got her voicemail. This time I left no message.

The next morning HSM's allotment gate was open and her shed empty. I called Celia immediately.

'It's OK,' she said. 'They're safe.'

'I met HSF last night,' I said. 'He was outside the gate.'

'What did you think of him?' Celia seemed genuinely interested.

'Well at first I thought he was lovely and then... I'm not sure what happened, but it was as if I was seeing him alongside her and the gap was too great: she's plain and hard-working and bloody infuriating but basically honest and decent and he's sexy and charming and far too sure of himself – and he didn't even know if this was where HSM had an allotment. Also, when I mentioned the police he ran away.'

Celia chuckled. 'I'll be there in ten minutes, put the kettle on.'

I'd brought along a box of lavender shortbread in case I found myself entertaining the children again, so by the time Celia turned up I had both tea and sustenance to offer in return for her story.

'When Janice left her children on the plot, she'd already moved out of the family home,' Celia explained.

'Why did she leave home and why did she abandon the children on the allotments?'

'HSF as you call him, or Frank Westall, as she called him, or Francis Western, or Frankie Westerman or any number of other names we've found out in the past couple of days, is an extremely unpleasant conman,' Celia said. 'He preys on women. He's almost certainly a bigamist.'

I sat back, sipping tea, waiting for a full explanation. Celia chewed shortbread in silence. Sometimes I wanted to throttle her! 'So how many other women were there?' I asked.

'Two that we know of. Which is to say that we found three wedding rings, one of which matched Janice's.'

'Found where?'

'When you told me what the kids were called, I knew there was something very odd going on, so I asked Janice what her husband did for a living.' Celia snagged another piece of shortbread without pausing for breath. 'And when she told me that he delivered luxury cars to their new owners, my suspicions were confirmed.'

'What have the kid's names got to do with anything?'

She sighed. 'Think about it.'

I thought. Nothing came to mind.

'Nope,' I said. 'I don't understand.'

'OK, try this, what's the oldest girl called?'

'Portia.'

'S.C.H.E.' Celia enunciated as if to the hard-of-hearing. 'Porsche.'

'Bloody hell! So Reatta…?'

'Also a car: a two-seater Buick, according to Stefan.'

'And Ayar?'

'Work it out for yourself,' she filled her mouth with shortbread.

'No! That's terrible!' The light was slow to dawn but dazzling when it did. 'He's called—'

'Yes!' She couldn't stop herself having the punchline. 'The poor little tyke's called Alfa Romeo!'

We laughed until we ached, until we cried, and then, when we stopped laughing, we stared at each other grimly.

'What a bastard,' I said.

'Absolutely.' Celia drained her tea. 'But Janice got some of her own back.'

'How come?'

'Well she knew, Frank is, or rather was, a salesman at a posh car showroom over in Kent. So Stefan and I drove up there and pretended we wanted to buy a classic car and have it driven to our place on the Costa Brava.'

'Do you have a place on the Costa Brava?'

'No, but Frank didn't know that. Stefan said he'd like to test the car on some country roads and he and Frank agreed to meet next day at a pub so they could do some rural driving. And when they met, Janice and I were watching from a dark corner of the lounge.'

'I don't see what difference that would make. She knew what he did for a living.'

'Yes, but *her* Frank didn't wear expensive designer clothes or a Rolex watch. Seeing him as he portrayed himself to Stefan was a shock to her. He'd been pretending he hated his job and was desperate to get enough money to leave it, but he didn't behave that way in the bar. Also, he flirted outrageously with the barmaid.'

'So what happened?'

'While they were out on their drive, Janice and I went back to the showroom. She confronted the owner. Apparently he'd met Frank's wife, and she wasn't Janice! So I suggested that we might take a look at Frank's desk, but it turns out he didn't have one. Guess what he did have?'

'I have no idea.'

'A locker. They all do, for storing clothing they wear when driving the cars to their new owners and so on. By now the showroom owner was quite nervy, so he asked us to wait in his office while he took advice from their lawyer.'

Celia stopped, drawing out the moment. I was desperate to know what had happened.

'The lawyer told the showroom owner that he shouldn't do anything unless Janice had evidence of wrongdoing, and we were getting nervous about Stefan and Frank coming back from their drive and finding us there, so we agreed nothing would be said to Frank and Janice would see if she could find anything that suggested Frank was actually breaking some law other than his marriage vows.'

'And did she?'

'Actually *I* did. It seemed to me that Frank was enough of a chancer to have a criminal record and when I googled him, it all came piling out. He'd pretended to share Janice's anti-capitalist beliefs and was taking her market money to buy a farm in Ireland where they would be able to live 'sustainably and sanely' without TV, radio, internet, cars and so on. But he had county court judgements against him, had been declared bankrupt numerous times and was being sought for maintenance by at least one former wife Janice knew nothing about. But it didn't matter anyway because Frank's boss was really spooked and during the evening he rang his other salesman to talk about Frank.'

'And?'

'And the other salesman said he was sure Frank was behaving badly in a number of ways, he knew that when Frank drove cars to their new owners he sometimes took off the expensive tyres and put cheap retreads on, selling the others for cash. He said nobody would have believed him because Frank was so charming. So the boss went back to the showroom and took the back off Frank's locker with a screwdriver and hammer.'

'So what happened when Frank got to work?'

Celia rubbed her face and I realised she was exhausted. 'Let me get it in the right order. Frank wasn't at home with Janice at that point. He'd told her he was driving a car to Denmark, which had made it all the more shocking to her to see him in a pub in Kent. She was very upset, so we went to the family home, gathered up the kids and some possessions and I took her to a flat in Newhaven belonging to a friend of ours. They needed a new tenant and Janice needed somewhere to feel safe while she sorted herself out.'

'What happened next?'

'Frank's boss made sure he was genuinely away, ringing him on his mobile and telling him to go straight off to collect a car from somewhere up North without coming in to work. Then he rang me, because Janice doesn't have a phone.'

'That must have made HSF's life easier,' I commented.

'For sure – she couldn't check up on him. Anyway, when Janice and I got back to the showroom we found the boss had laid out three wedding rings, a Rolex and a Breitling watch and several sets of house keys and credit cards and driving licences in different names on his desk.'

She took a deep breath. 'Then it all went a bit mad. The kids were at the flat, Janice was in tears, holding the ring that was the match to her own. The boss said he was sacking Frank immediately and Janice should take him to court for bigamy, and out she came with the announcement that they were married in the view of God, but not in church, so she had no legal standing. We all stood there staring at her like a bunch of sheep.'

'Typical HSM,' I said. 'Honest but maddening.'

Celia nodded. 'Exactly. There are times I want to shake her. Finally the boss took Janice outside and showed her a beautiful vintage Vespa scooter that he said was Frank's.'

I began to see what had happened next.

'The key to the scooter was in Frank's locker?'

'Indeed.'

'And then the scooter was on HSM's plot, behind that big wooden gate?'

'It was.'

'Is it worth much?'

Celia pursed her lips. 'Enough to get them started again somewhere else. Not enough to compensate for all the money he's taken from her. Nowhere near enough to make up for the life she's lived with him.'

'So the market stall was her way of trying to earn even more, so they could buy this farm in the country?'

'So she says. I can't help feeling that she was deliberately ignoring signs that things were wrong. She's not a stupid woman, but nobody wants to think they are being betrayed. My instinct is that she was trying to get enough money to help him escape the temptations that she knew, on some level, he was exposed to.'

'Poor HSM and poor kids.'

Celia stood and dusted down her jeans. 'We're auctioning the bike, but in Stefan's name. Frank can't do a thing about it because he's been sacked and his boss has told some of his creditors the address of the house. That's probably why he was outside the allotments: scared to go home in case the bailiffs got him.'

My head was reeling. 'So what happens now?'

'Janice and the kids are where he can't find them. She's put in for an allotment transfer and she's going wherever the first plot comes up. She's a free agent.'

I nodded, feeling miserable about the whole situation.

'According to his boss, Frank had a real thing for motorbikes and scooters,' Celia said.

'That's logical.' I was still thinking about the hard-working HSM and her shattered dreams.

'Why?'

'Well, there's always a risk when you play games like he did. You have to keep your story straight, make sure you wear the appropriate wedding ring, use the right endearments to the right woman and so on. But there are other risks too. Just being spotted by somebody who knows you from another life could destroy the whole illusion, so riding a motorbike or scooter is ideal – it means your face is covered and so there's much less chance of you being recognised.'

Celia nodded. 'That makes sense. I would never have thought of it though.' I preened myself until she added: 'I always knew you had a devious mind.'

If You Like Comfort Eating...

Comfort eating is what this book is all about, but not the slouched-on-the-sofa-with-a-tub-of-ice-cream kind of comfort, or kind of eating. I know allotment-holders like Chaz, who grow food to give it away, or Celia, who grow seeds and plants as a challenge or to keep viable seed in circulation for future generations, but while I applaud them, I don't understand them.

I grow food to eat. The crops I grow, by and large, are my favourites, and when I eat them I get two kinds of comfort: the satisfaction of palate and stomach is the first kind, but allied to that is the moral satisfaction of having produced good food from my own labour, without imposing much on the planet and with love for the little patch of ground that I call my own, although, in all kinds of ways, I'm only borrowing it. There's a spiritual reward, as well as a gustatory one, to eating something delicious that you first knew when it was a tiny seed.

Favourite foods vary from person to person. Mine include floury potatoes rather than waxy ones, yellow plums rather than red, and apples rather than pears – OH prefers strawberries to raspberries and pears to apples, which I find bizarre, but rather pleasing, as it means we don't compete to get the lion's share of our favourite foods.

Whatever our personal tastes, there tend to be common factors when it comes to comfort food. It's often substantial; it tends to remind us of a time in our lives when we were secure (usually childhood) and it is likely to have cultural connotations or traditional associations.

One of my comfort foods is hash – and to make a perfect hash, in my view, you need two vegetables: King Edward potatoes and purple sprouting broccoli.

Growing potatoes is a regional business. There aren't many crops that are as sensitive to soil and climate as the humble spud. In one way this is great, because there will definitely be a potato variety that grows well where you live, but it does make advising on potatoes tricky: what works for me in Sussex would be nonsense for a Fenlands grower, or somebody contending with the sandy earth of Surrey.

What everybody should do, regardless of location, is be sure not to plant potatoes in the same spot two years running, weed between potato rows with a hoe and draw up the soil regularly to protect the growing tubers from light which makes them green and toxic to the gut.

PURPLE SPROUTING
BROCCOLI HASH

INGREDIENTS

- King Edward potatoes
- Purple sprouting broccoli
- Onion

- Sunflower oil
- Leftovers from a previous meal (optional)
- Mushroom ketchup

METHOD

Boil some peeled and chunked King Edward potatoes for twenty minutes: for the last five minutes of cooking, place some purple sprouting broccoli stems in a steamer above the potatoes so they are just tender. Set the broccoli aside while you drain and mash the potatoes with some black pepper.

Slice and fry two onions in sunflower oil until brown and fragrant. You don't want to them to become crispy but you do need that rich dark aroma that onions give off when they are really well cooked.

If you prefer a vegetarian hash, tip the potato into the frying pan with the onions, give the whole mixture a good slosh of mushroom ketchup as you turn the potato over and over until it takes up the onions, and keep turning it as it browns, so that the ketchup is incorporated in the dish. If you are an omnivore, you can add a tin of corned beef, mashing it into the potato before adding to the frying pan, or some meat from a roast joint.

If you have gravy left over from a roast dinner, pour that into the frying pan too and allow it to mingle with the other ingredients. You can also use cold vegetables from Sunday lunch – just dice them to a regular size. Cook for around ten minutes, constantly lifting and turning the hash, and then add the broccoli stems, turning them gently into the mixture so they don't get broken up, but incorporating them carefully so that they become an integral part of the dish, like tasty fossils in a rock stratum.

This is a dish we love when we've come back from a tough winter's day digging. It's just as good on days we can't get to the plot: eaten with the rain beating down on the roof or when snow is on the ground, it can almost reconcile us to the miseries of bad weather.

If you're a fan of hearty comfort food like potato hash, apple pie may also float your comfort food boat. If so, you're not alone: on any number of internet lists and magazine 'top ten' pages you can find apple pie listed as a favourite comfort food. I suppose this is largely an American phenomenon, where pie = ultimate comfort, as in 'motherhood and apple pie', but there's another reason that apples feature highly in the recipes of those seeking an emotional haven. Apples have high amounts of quercetin, currently being explored as a contributor to human health in preventing degenerative mental conditions. Research at Cornell University suggests additional apple consumption may reduce the risk of neurodegenerative disorders such as Alzheimer's and Parkinson's disease – apples may indeed keep you happy, and healthy.

WINTER-STORED APPLE AND FROZEN BLACKBERRY *TARTE TATIN*

This is a particularly sumptuous winter dessert, adapted from a *tarte tatin* recipe in the cookbook *Chocolate & Zucchini*, by Clotilde Dusoulier. I've changed it so that it uses two different kinds of stored allotment produce: apples and blackberries.

This recipe will accommodate almost any apples: cookers (use more sugar) or eaters (use a little less), ones that pulp or ones that hold their shape, and can be made with pears too, although I think it is best with apples.

INGREDIENTS

PASTRY

- 170 grams plain flour
- 85 grams caster sugar
- 85 grams butter or cooking margarine
- 1 or 2 tablespoons milk

CARAMEL

- 85 grams demerara sugar for cooking apples, 60 grams for eating apples
- 1 tablespoon cold water
- 35 grams salted butter

FRUIT FILLING

• 1 kilogram apples

• 75 grams blackberries – either the last pick of the autumn, or some frozen ones

METHOD

Using a food processor, combine the butter and sugar, then add the flour and pulse until the mixture forms crumbs, at which point add a tablespoon of milk and pulse until a soft dough forms. If the dough doesn't swiftly come together into a ball, add a dash more milk. Then wrap the ball in clingfilm or pop it in a plastic bag and put it in the fridge for at least half an hour.

Grease a twenty-five centimetre cake tin and preheat the oven to 180°C (360°F).

While the oven is heating, make the caramel by putting the demerara sugar and water in a small heavy-bottomed saucepan. Put the pan on a medium to low heat, shaking from time to time to melt the sugar, but don't stir it. Once the mixture starts to boil allow it to cook for a minute or two until it caramelises. You'll know when because it becomes amber-coloured and smells deliciously toffee-like.

At this point, and before it starts to scorch, take the pan from the heat and beat the butter into the molten sugar. Pour this butterscotch-coloured cream into the tin and spread out with a spatula or the back of a metal spoon dipped in hot water. It doesn't have to reach right out to the edges of the dish because the pastry fits inside, over the top of the apples. Sprinkle the blackberries over the caramel.

Peel, core and slice the apples and lay neatly over the caramel and blackberries.

Remove the dough from the fridge, give it ten minutes to rest and then roll it out on a lightly floured surface. Because this dough is extremely fragile, I find it easier to flour a work surface, then lay clingfilm over the top of the dough and roll it out through the clingfilm. You need to make the pastry circle about five centimetres bigger than the base of the dish.

Fold the dough over the rolling pin to convey it to the dish. Lay it over the apples, sliding the edges of the dough in so that they rest between the apples and the sides of the dish and prick the top a couple of times with a fork. If the dough cracks a bit, don't worry – you can pinch it together with your fingers.

Put the dish on a middle shelf of the oven for fifty minutes to an hour, with a baking tray on the shelf below to catch any drips.

The tarte is cooked when the dough is golden and there's a superb smell of toffee apples.

Rest for five minutes before running a blunt knife around the inside of the dish to loosen the dough. Put a pretty plate, from which you wish to serve the tarte, over the top of the cooking dish. Flip the tarte dish over to serve.

This pudding is best served warm. We eat it with sour cream or crème fraîche because the sweetness of the fruit caramel doesn't need any further richness to complement it.

Endings and Beginnings

Allotment life is deeply seasonal. It restores the sense of living in harmony with nature in a way that has almost vanished from modern life. One aspect of this seasonality is that short days and bad weather lead to isolation. If you are working on your plot in winter, you may not see another allotment-holder all day, while in summer, if you're on plot for an hour or two, you'll see loads of people wandering by. In the few days that were fit for allotment work that November I saw almost nobody, and was happy enough to make the most of the hours in which I could dig, make bonfires to burn prunings from the fruit trees, and plan my planting for the year ahead.

It was several weeks before I saw Celia again and she told me that HSM had moved to the north of the county, where Ayar had been enrolled in a primary school and the two girls were joining the Guides to get them used to structured time with other children before deciding if they too wanted to try going to school.

In December I found myself at a Christmas market. I'd been meeting a new client who wanted me to write a weekly blog about 'the excitement of owning a bath hoist': an idea that was struggling to gain purchase in my imagination. I drifted into the market looking for sustenance while I tried to organise my thoughts in such a way that 'excitement' and 'bath hoist' could become congruent. I bought a pasty and tried to find somewhere to sit down. A tall, thin girl, giggling with her friends, made space for me on a bench and then tapped me on the knee.

'You don't recognise me, do you?' she said. 'You're the Parsnip Lady.'

I stared at her. 'Your mum used to have an allotment near mine, didn't she?'

The girl was transformed. Her hair was straight and quite possibly highlighted, there was glittery nail polish on her fingers and she was wearing pink training shoes.

'That's right. Portia, like in Shakespeare.'

I took the hint. 'How's your mum and your brother and sister?'

'Mum's great. Rhiannon and Andy are fine too.'

Rhiannon and Andy. Well, well! I smiled at her and she blushed. 'Thank you for taking care of us that day. Mum was very grateful.'

'That's OK, I'm glad to see you looking so...' I wasn't sure what to say, so I just stuck up my thumb.

'Would you like to say hello to Mum? She's due for a break about now.'

Portia led the way between market stalls, chattering away, 'She's running a community garden for people with learning disabilities – some work in the garden, some make food in the kitchens and some sell the produce at markets like this one. She's really good at it.'

'And are you going to school?'

'Yeah, of course. We couldn't stay home once she got a job. We all go to school now. Rhiannon hates it, but Andy thinks it's better than TV. There's Mum now.'

She pointed, and I saw a woman in the mid distance, laughing as she tried to shove an immense Savoy cabbage into a rather too small carrier bag. Her long red hair was twisted in a knot above the turned-up collar of a leopard-skin jacket.

'*That's* your mother?'

Portia grinned. 'I help her do her hair every month; the roots show something awful. She looks dead nice as a redhead though, doesn't she?'

I nodded. It seemed to me that HSM probably didn't want to be reminded of her past, and certainly didn't need to be interrupted by an unwelcome visitor in the middle of her busy day.

'Actually Portia, I don't think I have time right now. Tell your mum I said hello, and I'm glad she's doing so well.'

I turned and walked away.

Several months later HSM's plot had been divided and two families were working, somewhat ineptly, the soil she'd managed with such love and care. One family had built a bog garden in half a water butt. They'd bought it for a tenner from Felix, who'd bought it back from Compact and Bijou for a pound when the committee insisted they improve their cultivation percentage and take out some of their kitsch features.

Spring was heading towards summer and Rebus was temporarily banned from the allotments because the vixen was raising fox cubs under the shed two plots along from 'Nearly' and they liked to use the lid of our cold frame as a vantage point to ambush each other. Even the best-behaved terrier would view high-level fox cubs as an incitement to violence.

Our greenhouse was full of plants and the broad beans were thrumming with bees. Everything was wonderful, until I looked up and saw the committee standing at the boundary of my plot.

'We've got some bad news,' I was told and braced myself to learn that I was about to be evicted from 'Nearly' for as-yet-unrevealed transgressions. 'You've reached the top of the list.'

I blinked. 'Why is that bad news?'

'Because you don't have to be secretary any more if you don't want to.'

The committee took me on a tour of the available sites, all half-plots, and I picked out one that had a good path and a decent shed, friable soil and nice neighbours. It would be sad to give up 'Nearly', particularly for a smaller growing space, but there wasn't any alternative if we wanted to secure a plot of our own.

On the way to the office to sign the tenancy agreement I passed Felix.

'I'm at the top of the waiting list! I've got a plot of my own at last!' I half-shouted, excited by my good fortune.

He smiled. 'They haven't fobbed you off with that pagan plot, have they?'

I stopped. 'Pagan plot?'

'You know, the one with the oaks and elder trees and the crop circles.'

'Show me!'

Felix led the way to a plot I had never noticed before, so thick were its rose-briar hedges, studded with gooseberry bushes at the base and twined with bindweed at the top so that icy white trumpets nodded above our heads.

He was right about the oaks: two of them, although they weren't very tall, and the elder, which was multi-trunked, heavy with flowers and right in the middle of the plot, reducing the cultivable land by around a fifth. What little planting I could see was indeed circular, as was the firepit, which was big enough to hold an ox. Grasshoppers fell silent as I pushed my way up the path and a lizard ran across the bricks in the fireplace. At the back of the plot there were two sheds and a glasshouse containing an old, dead, gnarled vine studded with dolls' heads. It was indeed pagan, and very creepy.

'They can't get anybody to take this one: not even complete beginners are stupid enough to try and get it back into cultivation,' Felix shouted from the gate.

I pushed open the glasshouse door. Inside were around a hundred wooden walking sticks and some mirrors. A lot of mirrors. A wren peered out of its nest in a huge bay tree as if it had never seen a human being before. Judging by the height of the grass, the age of the vine and the thick mulch of leaves under the fruit trees, that was entirely possible. Opposite the firepit was a mound of honeysuckle about two metres tall which looked as if could have been hiding a wicker man.

'You'd have to be completely mental to choose a plot like that,' Felix said as I wandered back down the path.

'Hmmm,' I said. I walked down to the office, then went home via the supermarket. I needed to buy some ingredients for dinner.

When OH got home I told him the good news. 'I reached the top of the waiting list.'

He sniffed the air. 'Steak and kidney. I'm not going to like what comes next, am I?'

'Eat your dinner,' I said. 'I'll tell you about it afterwards. But let's just say we've got a lovely... opportunity.'

THE
WALKER'S
FRIEND

A MISCELLANY OF
WIT AND WISDOM

JUDE PALMER

THE WALKER'S FRIEND

A MISCELLANY OF WIT AND WISDOM

Jude Palmer

ISBN: 978-1-84953-052-1   Hardback   £9.99

'I have two doctors, my left leg and my right'   G. M. Trevelyan

As Henry David Thoreau said, an early morning walk is a blessing for the whole day – a time to breathe fresh air and feel the grass under your feet, replenish the spirits and calm the mind, and let the thoughts flow while enjoying nature's bounteous pleasures.

Hikers, ramblers, dog walkers and casual strollers will savour this beautifully designed collection of quotations and excerpts from classic and contemporary writing, both humorous and evocative, interspersed with practical tips on everything from walking boots to where to spot wildlife.

'This is a charming book for all lovers of walking and the countryside... intended to remind everyone of the myriad pleasures of walking'
WILDLIFE magazine

'an ideal gift for anyone with an interest in walking'
SCOTTISH HOME AND COUNTRY magazine

TRUGS
DIBBERS
TROWELS
AND
TWINE and everything

good about GARDENING
with little TIPS and
words of WISDOM and
INSPIRATION on the simplest
of pleasures

ISOBEL CARLSON

TRUGS, DIBBERS, TROWELS AND TWINE

Isobel Carlson

ISBN: 978-1-84953-040-8   Hardback   £9.99

'All the flowers of all the tomorrows are in the seeds of today'
Indian proverb

Follow the garden path to horticultural heaven with this satisfying harvest of garden wisdom. Whether you are in need of some blossoming inspiration or your fingers are the colour of freshly mown grass, this compendium of gardening advice is overflowing with both classic and contemporary tips for making your garden grow and fascinating snippets of garden folklore. Learn about:

• recycling old household items

• how to keep out bugs and slugs and attract valuable creatures in

• why you should always keep a leek in your attic and never kill a ladybird.

'a wonderful collection of garden wisdom'   CHOICE magazine

'A great gift. Full of tips and folklore'   GOOD HOMES magazine

'For a quirky take on garden wit and wisdom, look no further'
SCOTLAND ON SUNDAY

Gardening Wit

Quips and Quotes for the Green-Fingered

Jane Brook

GARDENING WIT

QUIPS AND QUOTES FOR THE GREEN-FINGERED

Jane Brook

ISBN: 978-1-84024-786-2   Hardback   £9.99

'To turn ordinary clothes into gardening clothes, simply mix with compost'
Guy Browning

'Every man reaps what he sows in this life – except the amateur gardener'
Lesley Hall

After a long day of digging and planting, throw in the trowel and enjoy a little light weeding from this stupendous harvest of quips and quotes from those who really know their onions.

Green-fingered gurus and nature-loving novices need look no further to find a saying for every season.

'just the book to dip into when you're having a well-earned break or need a spot of light bedtime reading' **GARDEN NEWS**

Have you enjoyed this book?
If so, why not write a review on your favourite website?

Thanks very much for buying this Summersdale book.

www.summersdale.com